APOLOGETICS
FOR A
New Generation

Sean
McDowell
GENERAL EDITOR

HARVEST HOUSE PUBLISHERS
EUGENE, OREGON

Cover by Abris, Veneta, Oregon

Cover photo © Ryan Klos / iStockphoto.com

Sean McDowell: This Work published in association with the Conversant Media Group, P.O. Box 3006, Redmond, WA, 98007.

ConversantLife.com is a registered trademark of Conversant Media Group. Harvest House Publishers, Inc., is a licensee of the federally registered trademark ConversantLife.com.

APOLOGETICS FOR A NEW GENERATION
Copyright © 2009 by Sean McDowell
Published by Harvest House Publishers
Eugene, Oregon 97402
www.harvesthousepublishers.com

Library of Congress Cataloging-in-Publication Data
Apologetics for a new generation / Sean McDowell, general editor.
    p. cm.—(ConversantLife.com)
    ISBN 978-0-7369-2520-4 (pbk.)
    1. Apologetics. I. McDowell, Sean.
    BT1103.A66 2009
    239—dc22

                                                                2008038016

Printed in the United States of America

16 17 / VP-SK / 12 11 10

Download a Deeper Experience

Sean McDowell is part of a faith-based online community called ConversantLife.com. At this Web site, people engage their faith in entertainment, creative arts, science and technology, global concerns, and other culturally relevant topics. While you're reading this book, or after you have finished reading, go to www.conversantlife.com/seanmcdowell and use these icons to read and download additional material from Sean that is related to the book.

Resources: Download study guide materials for personal devotions or a small-group Bible study.

Videos: Click on this icon for interviews with Sean and video clips on various topics.

Blogs: Read through Sean's blogs and articles and comment on them.

Podcasts: Stream ConversantLife.com podcasts and audio clips from Sean.

conversant life .com

engage your faith

To my daughter, Shauna—
I pray that you will be a voice of love
and truth to your generation

Acknowledgments

My deep gratitude goes to each of the writers who contributed to this book. Thank you for your willingness to be part of this project, but even more for your passionate commitment to reaching a new generation. In particular, I appreciate Brett Kunkle's encouragement and insights as I first started to dream about this book.

Thanks to Stan Jantz and Bruce Bickel for believing in this project and helping to make it a reality. Conversantlife.com is a great vision that I am honored to be part of! And thanks to Terry Glaspey for helping make *Apologetics for a New Generation* appealing to as wide an audience as possible.

Finally, I am honored to partner once again with the team at Harvest House. Thank you for believing in this project and for your vision to effectively reach new generations for Christ.

CONTENTS

FOREWORD

by David Kinnaman

D oes the advice dispensed by so-called experts ever seem confusing?

Some say you should adapt your ministry to a completely
unique, distinct generation. Or is it more accurate to say that young
people today are not that different from previous generations? Do we
need new ways of thinking and innovative approaches to engage the
emerging generation, or should we dig deeper into the past to find
answers in our history and traditions?

Everything is changing—or is nothing new?

Reality is less clear-cut than we like, isn't it? Apologetics is no different; it is hard, soul-bending, head-scratching work. The book you
are holding, *Apologetics for a New Generation,* helped me wrestle with
the complexities of apologetics in a changing context. It gave me new
ideas, new language, and new thinking while grounding those concepts squarely in biblical truths. My friend Sean McDowell has done
a masterful job of blending the voices of experts, thinkers, theologians,
and practitioners into a book that is not just a compilation of academic
perspectives. Instead, it is a book of solid thinking and sound ideas—
concepts you will come back to again and again but that you can put
into practice right away.

To kick things off, let me offer four perspectives that may shape
your reading. First, realize that we live in an era of change. God does
not change, but human culture does. You may be tempted to read this
book with an eye on the past, but digest it with a sense of what God
is doing now and in the future. We can't use apologetics to pound a

generation into submission; we *can* use it to prepare young people for the great things God has planned for them.

Second, put this book to work. Use it to make specific changes to your ministry. You probably have your own style of reading books, but I urge you to let this book serve as more than a mere intellectual journey. Pick out favorite chapters (I have). Come back to them and wrestle with them. Start a book discussion group. Write out things you agree with and those you disagree with. Keep asking yourself, so what? Then answer the so-what question by listing what the insights mean for your ministry. This book is important, but even more crucial is the outcome: rethinking and retooling your ministry to young people when it comes to apologetics.

Third, do not underestimate the importance of connecting apologetics to this generation's skepticism, but not as in *Question X = Answer Y.* Young people want to converse. They love to question things. This goes beyond the typical adolescent impulse to reject the views of older adults; this generation has been raised to discuss (and distrust) *everything.* Apologetics is changing because young people are resistant to mere intellectual arguments, yet they seem to be as open as any generation to meaningful, transparent, long-term, and loving relationships. Our research confirms this over and over: Relationships are the nuts and bolts of spiritual conversations, spiritual conversions, and spiritual maturation. You will find this idea threaded throughout this volume.

And that leads to the fourth aspect of this book you should know about. This book does not just talk about the importance of a relational approach to apologetics. It is birthed out of relationships. Sean McDowell has invited writers to participate not just because they are experts, but because they work with young people. More than that, these writers are Sean's friends and colleagues. In fact, Sean and I share a connection too: We lived in the same dormitory at Biola. He put everything he had into life, basketball, and studies. It's the same approach he takes now as he works with this next generation.

And, of course, don't forget Sean's relationship with his dad, Josh

McDowell—legendary apologist. This book (and Sean's ministry) is a testament to a father getting it right in the most important earthly relationship of his life. Josh came to speak at Biola when Sean and I were at the tail end of our time at the university. Before Josh began speaking, he asked his son to stand up in the huge crowd. "You are my most important ministry, Sean. And I am so proud of you and the kind of man you have become," he said. It wasn't just words. Despite his ministry schedule and commitments, Josh had appeared at Sean's basketball games and was clearly an active supporter of Sean in all the appropriate ways. Read between the lines in this book. You and I are benefiting from a relational apologetic at work, father to son.

Just like relationships, apologetics is a tricky and confusing business. Which experts do you believe? Is apologetics with young people more important than ever or less so? Or, like Sean and his team of writers ask, do we need a *new kind* of apologetic?

Let this terrific book be your guide to classic questions and fresh answers.

David Kinnaman is president of the Barna Group and the author of *unChristian: What a New Generation Really Thinks About Christianity.*

APOLOGETICS FOR A NEW GENERATION

by Sean McDowell

The voice on the other end of the phone was familiar, but the question took me by complete surprise. "You teach your students to defend their faith, right?" asked John, a close friend of mine. "Tell me, how do you know Christianity is true?" John and I have had a special relationship for more than a decade, but this was the first time he had shown any real interest in spiritual matters. And he not only wanted to talk about God, he wanted an apologetic for the faith—he wanted proof, reason, and evidence before he would consider believing. John later told me his interest in God was piqued when his younger brother was diagnosed with a brain tumor at 16 years old. His younger brother has since had surgery and experienced complete recovery. In John's own words, this experience "woke him up to his own mortality."

A few weeks after our phone conversation, John was heading back to school in northern California, so we decided to meet for a chat over coffee. As we sat down at the Starbucks across from the historic San Juan Capistrano Mission, John jumped right in. "I'm scientific minded, so I need some evidence for the existence of God and the accuracy of the Bible. What can you show me?" For the next hour and a half we discussed some of the standard arguments for the existence of God, the historical evidence for the death and resurrection of Jesus, and the basis for the reliability of the Bible. I did my best to answer his questions, trying to show that Christianity is rationally compelling and provides the most satisfying solution to the deepest longings of the heart. John didn't become a Christian at this point, but he confessed that he was very close and just needed more time to weigh the cost of his decision.

When I reflected on this discussion, comments I have heard over the past decade by young leaders came rushing to my mind:

"We live in a postmodern era, so apologetics is not important anymore."

"Young people no longer care about reasons for the existence of the Christian God. What matters is telling your narrative and being authentic."

"New generations today no longer need 'evidence that demands a verdict' or a 'case for Christ.'"

"Conversion is about the heart, not the intellect."

Of course, these statements are oversimplifications. Still, we must ask, is scientific proof an important part of faith? Do we live in an era in which people still have questions that demand a truth-related response? Is John the exception, the norm, or somewhere in between? If we are going to be effective in reaching a new generation of young people, few questions, it would seem, are more pressing and important than these.

Postmodernism

In the early 1990s, interest in postmodernism exploded in the church. Bestselling books and popular conferences featured seminars about doing ministry in a postmodern world. People disagreed about exactly what is meant by "postmodernism"—and they still do!—but many agreed that the world was leaving the modern era behind and wading into the unknown waters of the postmodern matrix.

According to many, postmodernism marks the most important cultural shift of the past 500 years, upending our theology, philosophy, epistemology (how we know things), and church practice. Some compare postmodernism to an earthquake that has overturned all the foundations of Western culture. Thus, to be relevant in ministry today, we must shed our modern tendencies and embrace the postmodern shift. According to many postmoderns, this shift includes replacing a propositional approach to the gospel with a primarily relational methodology.

To be honest, for the past 15 years I have wrestled profoundly with this so-called postmodern shift, reading books about postmodernism, attending conferences, and engaging in endless conversations with both Christians and non-Christians about the state of culture today. As much as the next guy, I want my life and ministry to be biblically grounded and culturally relevant. If the world is really undergoing a profound shift, I want to embrace it!

The world is certainly changing fast. Advancements in technology, transportation, and communication are taking place at an unprecedented rate. But what does this *really* mean for ministry today? Certainly, as postmoderns like to emphasize, story, image, and community are critical components. But does it follow that we downplay reason, evidence, and apologetics? Absolutely not! In fact, as the contributors to this book all agree, apologetics is more important than ever before.

Postmodern ideas do influence the worldview of youth today, but their thinking is most deeply influenced by our predominantly modern, secular culture. This can be seen most clearly by comparing the way they think about religion and ethics with the way they think about science. Youth are significantly relativistic when it comes to ethics, values, and religion, but they are *not* relativistic about science, mathematics, and technology.[1] This is because they have grown up in a secular culture that deems science as the superior means of attaining knowledge about the world. In *Kingdom Triangle,* philosopher J.P. Moreland writes, "Scientific knowledge is taken to be so vastly superior that its claims always trump the claims made by other disciplines."[2] Religion and morals, on the other hand, are considered matters of personal preference and taste over which the individual is autonomous. This is why, if you've had a discussion with a younger person, you've probably heard her say, "That may be true for you, but it's not true for me," "Who are you to judge?" or "If that's what they choose, whatever." This is not because of their postmodern sentiments, but because their thinking has been profoundly shaped by their modernist and secular culture.

Popular writers such as Christopher Hitchens, Sam Harris, and Richard Dawkins have written bestselling books attacking the scientific, historic, and philosophical credibility of religion in general and Christianity in particular.[3] Their writings have wreaked havoc on many unprepared Christians. This has taken place while many inside the church have neglected the need to be able to defend the faith intellectually. Christians today are regularly being challenged to set forth the reasons for their hope. And with the ubiquity of the Internet, difficult questions seem to be arising now more than ever before. As professor David Berlinski writes in *The Devil's Delusion:* "The question that all religious believers now face: Show me the evidence."[4]

I am convinced that C.S. Lewis was right: The question is not really *if* we will defend the Christian faith, but if we will defend it *well*. Whether we like it or not, we are all apologists of a sort.

The Apologetics Renaissance

During research for *The Case for Christ,* Lee Strobel was told by a well-known and respected theologian that no one would read his book. Lee was informed, "People don't care about historical evidence for Jesus anymore. They're more persuaded by experience and community than facts and reason." Disappointed and frustrated, Lee returned home and told his wife that his efforts were seemingly in vain. Yet according to Lee, the largest group of readers who became Christians through his book has been 16- to 24-year-olds!

Philosopher William Lane Craig's 2008 cover story for *Christianity Today,* "God Is Not Dead Yet: How Current Philosophers Argue for His Existence," is a sign of things to come. Craig ties the awakening of apologetics to the renaissance in Christian philosophy that has taken place over the past 40 years. Science is more open to the existence of a Designer than at any time in recent memory (thanks to the intelligent design movement), and biblical criticism has embarked on a renewed quest for the historical Jesus consonant with the portrait of Jesus found in the Gospels.[5]

The apologetics awakening can also be seen in the number of apologetics conferences that have sprouted up in churches all over the country. Tens of thousands of people are trained at apologetics events through efforts of various church denominations and organizations, such as Biola University, Southern Evangelical Seminary, Focus on the Family, and more. Resources on apologetics have also exploded in the past few years. This is good news because America and the church continue to become more and more secular. Those who describe themselves as "religious nonaffiliated" have increased from 5 to 7 percent in the 1970s to 17 percent in 2006.[6]

Why Apologetics Matters

To say that apologetics is critical for ministry today is not to say that we just continue business as usual. That would be foolish. Our world is changing, and it is changing *rapidly*. More change has happened since 1900 than in all prior recorded history. And more change will occur in the next 20 years than the entire last century.[7] But God does not change (Malachi 3), and neither does human nature. We are thoughtful and rational beings who respond to evidence. People have questions, and we are responsible to provide helpful answers. Of course, we certainly don't have all the answers, and when we do provide solid answers, many choose not to follow the evidence for personal or moral reasons. But that hardly changes the fact that we are rational, personal beings who bear the image of God.

People often confuse apologetics with apologizing for the faith, but the Greek word *apologia* refers to a legal defense. Thus, apologetics involves giving a defense for the Christian faith. First Peter 3:15 says, "Sanctify Christ as Lord in your hearts, always being ready to make a defense [*apologia*] to everyone who asks you to give an account for the hope that is in you, yet with gentleness and respect." Jude encouraged his hearers to "contend earnestly for the faith which was once for all handed down to the saints" (Jude 3). The biblical evidence is clear: All Christians are to be trained in apologetics, which is an integral part of discipleship. This involves learning how to respond to common objections raised against the Christian faith and also how to positively commend the gospel to a particular audience.

We have certainly made mistakes in the way we have defended our beliefs in the past (as chapters in this book will illustrate), but this hardly means we should abandon apologetics altogether. Rather, we ought to learn from the past and adjust accordingly. Beyond the biblical mandate, apologetics is vitally important today for two reasons.

Strengthening Believers

Apologetics training can offer significant benefits in the personal life of Christians. For one thing, knowing *why* you believe *what* you believe and experiencing it in your life and relationships will give you renewed confidence in sharing your faith. I have the privilege of speaking to thousands of young people every year. Inevitably, whenever I speak on topics such as moral relativism, the case for intelligent design, or evidences for the resurrection, I get e-mails and comments on my Facebook page from students who were strengthened in their faith. One recently wrote, "I was at the [youth event] this past weekend and absolutely loved it! All the information was so helpful, but I connected the most with yours. All the scientific proof of Christianity and a Creator just absolutely amazes me!"

Training in apologetics also provides an anchor during trials and difficulties. Emotions only take us so far, and then we need something more solid. Presently, most teens who enter adulthood claiming to be Christians will walk away from the church and put their emotional commitment to Christ on the shelf within ten years.[8] A young person may walk away from God for many reasons, but *one* significant reason is intellectual doubt. According to the National Study of Youth and Religion, the most common answer nonreligious teens offered for why they left their faith was intellectual skepticism.[9] This is why David Kinnaman, president of the Barna Group, writes in his book *unChristian,*

"We are learning that one of the primary reasons that ministry to teenagers fails to produce a lasting faith is because they are not being taught to think."[10]

The church is failing young people today. From the moment Christian students first arrive on campus, their faith is assaulted on all sides by fellow students and teachers alike. According to a ground-breaking 2006 study by professors from Harvard and George Mason universities, the percentage of agnostics and atheists teaching at American colleges is three times greater than in the general population. More than 50 percent of college professors believe the Bible is "an ancient book of fables, legends, history, and moral precepts."[11] Students are routinely taught that Darwinian evolution is the substitute creator, that the Bible is unreliable, that Jesus was like any other religious figure, and that any Christian who thinks differently is at best old-fashioned and at worst intolerant, bigoted, and hateful. These ideas are perpetrated in the classroom through reason, logic, and evidence. The church must teach students to counter these trends.

This was exactly the experience of Alison Thomas, a recent seminary grad who is now a speaker for Ravi Zacharias Ministries (and the author of the chapter "Apologetics and Race"). As a college freshman, her faith was immediately attacked from every direction. Combine the intellectual challenges with the lack of nutrition, sleep, and Christian mentors, and according to Alison, it was a recipe for disaster: "I almost abandoned my faith in college because I was not sure if the difficult questions people asked me about Christianity had satisfying answers."[12] Alison is absolutely convinced that had she been prepared for the attack on her faith, she could have been spared much doubt, sin, and heartache. Her story could be multiplied thousands of times, but unfortunately, too often with different results.

Reaching the Lost

The apostles of Christ ministered in a pluralistic culture. They regularly reasoned with both Jews and pagans, trying to persuade them of the truth of Christianity. They appealed to fulfilled prophecy, Jesus' miracles, evidence for creation, and proofs for the resurrection. Acts 17:2-3 says, "And according to Paul's custom, he went to them, and for three Sabbaths reasoned with them from the Scriptures, explaining and giving evidence that the Christ had to suffer and rise again from the dead, and saying, 'This Jesus whom I am proclaiming to you is the Christ.'" Some were persuaded as a result of Paul's efforts.

According to pastor Tim Keller, this is similar to the method we should adopt today. Keller is the avant-garde pastor of Redeemed Presbyterian Church in Manhattan and the author of *The Reason for God*, an apologetics book which has soared atop the *New York Times* bestselling nonfiction list. In an interview for *Christianity Today*, Keller responded to the claim that rationality is unimportant for evangelism: "Christians are saying that the rational isn't part of evangelism. The fact is, people are rational. They do have questions. You have to answer those questions. Don't get the impression that I think that the rational aspect takes you all the way there. But there's too much emphasis on just the personal now."[13] Tim is right: Evangelism today must be both relational and rational.

Greg Stier agrees: "Any claims concerning the death of apologetics have been greatly exaggerated...Those who believe apologetics aren't important for evangelizing postmoderns have misdiagnosed this generation as purely relational; these young people are rational, too."[14] According to Greg, this generation of young people is more open to spiritual truth than any generation in recent history. (See my brief interview with him on page 124.)

Does this mean young people are walking around with deep spiritual questions at the forefront of their minds? Not necessarily. But it does mean that many young people are open to spiritual truth when motivated in the right way. The problem is not with apologetics but with our failure to motivate people. Much ministry today is focused on meeting a felt need, but the real difficulty is to take a genuine need and make it felt. If done in the context of a relationship, apologetics can be one effective means of accomplishing this. For thoughts on how to motivate young people in this regard see the chapter "Making Apologetics Come Alive in Youth Ministry" by Alex McFarland.

In my experience, people who criticize apologetics have often had one or two unsuccessful attempts and written off the entire enterprise. Rather, we need to put apologetics into perspective. Considering that a minority of people who hear the gospel choose to become followers of Christ in the first place, we shouldn't be surprised that many people are unmoved by reason and evidence. It's unrealistic to expect most people to respond positively to apologetics, just as it is unrealistic to expect most people to respond to a presentation of the gospel. The road is narrow in both cases (Matthew 7:14).

If only a few people will respond, why bother? For one thing, those who respond to apologetics often become people of significant influence who are deeply committed to the faith. This has certainly been the case in the life of my father, Josh McDowell. He became a believer as a pre-law student while trying to refute the evidence for Christ. I'm deeply humbled by the number of doctors, professors, politicians, lawyers, and other influential professionals who have come to Christ through his speaking and writing. He has spoken to more young people than anyone in history, and his books have been printed in millions of copies and translated all over the world. Honestly, I can hardly speak anywhere without someone from the audience sharing how instrumental he was in his or her coming to Christ. I'm proud to be his son.

Apologetics for a New Generation

Apologetics is advancing like never before, and a few characteristics mark effective apologetics for a new generation.

The New Apologetics Is Missional

There is a lot of talk right now about being missional, that is, getting out of our safe Christian enclaves and reaching people on their turf. This mind-set must characterize apologetics for a new generation. Each spring Brett Kunkle and I take a group of high school students to the

University of California at Berkeley to interact with leading atheists from northern California. We invite various speakers to challenge our students and then to participate in a lively period of questions and answers. The guests always comment that our students treat them kindly, ask good questions, and are different from stereotypical Christians. This is because, in our preparatory training, we emphasize the importance of defending our beliefs with gentleness and respect, as Peter admonishes (1 Peter 3:15).

In Western culture today, Christians are often criticized for being exclusive, closed-minded, and intolerant. Missional apologetics is one way to help shatter this myth firsthand. Interestingly, one of the atheistic presenters from Berkeley spent 45 minutes arguing that the skeptical way of life is the most open-minded and the least dogmatic. I kindly pointed out that it was us—*Christians!*—who were willing to come up to their turf and give them a platform to present their ideas.

This is not the only perception of Christians that can be softened by missional apologetics. In his book *unChristian,* David Kinnaman paints a sobering view of how Christians are viewed by those outside the faith. For example, nearly half of young non-Christians have a negative view of evangelicals. Six common perceptions characterize how young outsiders view Christians: hypocritical, too focused on getting converts, anti-homosexual, sheltered, too political, and judgmental.[15] To help overcome these perceptions, says Kinnaman, Christians must build meaningful, genuine relationships with non-Christians and live out their faith consistently. It is in the context of a loving relationship, says Dan Kimball in his chapter, "A New Kind of Apologist," that we most effectively reach the lost today.

The New Apologetics Influences How We Live

Though I do not agree with his philosophy of pragmatism, one insight of William James has practical importance for apologetics training today. James said that when considering any idea, we should always ask, what difference does it make? If it makes no existential difference to the way we live whether it is true or false, then according to James, we should not bother with it. When training in apologetics, we must regularly ask, so what? How does belief in the historical resurrection of Jesus affect my relationship to myself, to others, and to God? How does belief in creation influence my view of the environment? How does the Incarnation affect my self-image?

Much of the criticism today is not with apologetics per se but with our failure to connect apologetics to the way we live. Some of this criticism is deserved. If we don't apply the truth to our relationship with God and others, what's the point? Brian McLaren, a leading voice in the Emergent church, is right: Having right answers that don't lead us to better love God and our neighbors are more or less worthless.[16]

A remarkable number of outspoken critics of Christianity have backgrounds of personal disappointment with Christians and the church. Pastor Tim Keller explains how our personal experience influences our evaluation of the evidence for Christianity:

> We all bring to issues intellectual predispositions based on our experiences. If you have known many wise, loving, kind, and insightful Christians over the years, and if you have seen churches that are devout in belief yet civic-minded and generous, you will find the intellectual case for Christianity more plausible. If, on the other hand, the preponderance of your experience is with nominal Christians (who bear the name but don't practice) or with self-righteous fanatics, then the arguments for Christianity will have to be extremely strong for you to concede that they have any cogency at all.[17]

The great philosopher Frederick Nietzsche once commented that Christians have no joy. No wonder he found the evidence for God unconvincing. The sad part about his observation is that Christians, of all people, have the best reason to be joyful. If Christ has not risen, says Paul, "Let us eat and drink, for tomorrow we die" (1 Corinthians 15:32). But if Christ *has* risen—and the evidence for this is compelling—then even though we go through pain and difficulty in this life, we will share eternity with Him. Christians joyfully living out their faith in the power of the Holy Spirit provide one of the most powerful apologetics at our disposal.

The New Apologetics Is Humble

I failed miserably to act humbly a few years ago when getting my hair cut in Breckenridge, Colorado. The hairdresser noticed I was carrying a copy of *The Gospel in a Pluralist Society* by Leslie Newbigin. So she asked, "Are you a Christian? If so, how can you explain all the evil in the world?" I proceeded to give her a ten-minute lecture about the origin of evil, the nature of free will, and the Christian solution. My reasons were solid, but I lacked humility and sensitivity in my demeanor. I had a slick answer to her every question, but I missed the fact that her needs went beyond the intellect to her heart. Eventually she started crying—not because she became a Christian but because she was so offended by my callousness. To be honest, it was a bit unsettling having a hairdresser, who held sharp scissors in her hand, crying and lecturing me while cutting my hair. But the point was well taken.

In retrospect, I should have first asked her some questions to try and understand why evil was such a pressing issue in her life. What pain had she experienced that caused her to question the goodness of God? Sometimes questions are primarily intellectual, but more often than not they stem from a deeper longing of the heart.

From the beginning, Christian apologists have exemplified the importance of humility in presenting our defense of the faith. There is a reason why 1 Peter 3:15 begins with "Sanctify Christ as Lord in your hearts" and ends with "gentleness and respect." Before presenting a case for the Christian faith, one must first submit to the lordship of Christ. The heart of the apologist is the basis of all apologetic training. People still don't care how much you know if they don't know you care. The only way we can truly demonstrate the love of Christ to people is by first having our hearts humbled by God. When our hearts are not right, we can do more harm than good.

As you will see throughout this book, these are not the only factors characterizing the emerging apologetics awakening. The rest of the chapters in this book will spur you to think creatively about how apologetics fits into the many critical components of effective ministry today. Authors will tackle issues such as race, gender, media, homosexuality, Jesus, brain research, culture, youth, spiritual formation, and more—all with an eye on how we can effectively minister to new generations today.

Conclusion

In the fall of 2007, Christianity Today International and Zondervan partnered to conduct attitudinal and behavioral research of American Christians. *Leadership Journal* discussed the findings with leading pastors and religious experts to ascertain implications for ministry today. Three critical issues emerged:

1. The local church is no longer considered the only outlet for spiritual growth.

2. Churches must develop relational and community-oriented outreach.

3. Lay people have to be better equipped to be God's ambassadors [apologists].[18]

The third point on this list took me by surprise, not because I disagree with it, but because it's refreshing to hear leaders emphasize the renewed need for apologetics. In the article, Joel Hunter, senior pastor of Northland church in Longwood, Florida, said, "We need to preach with apologetics in mind, with a rational explanation and defense of the Christian faith in mind."[19] One of the best ways to counter biblical illiteracy, claims Hunter, is to equip active Christians as teachers, ambassadors, and apologists. Yes! Ministry today certainly includes much more than presenting a case for our hope, but this is one critical piece we must not neglect. The time has never been greater for a renewed focus on apologetics.

You may be wondering what happened to John, my friend I mentioned at the beginning of the chapter. He has not become a Christian yet, but he is still inching along. We continue to have good discussions about God and the meaning of life. I trust and pray that someday he will choose to follow Jesus. Had my youth pastor, parents, and teachers not trained me in apologetics, I couldn't have helped him at all. You and I can't be ambassadors without having answers to tough questions. So I've assembled this team of (mostly) young apologists to help you develop a biblical and culturally relevant approach for reaching this new generation. Let's go!

Part I

A NEW APPROACH

Christians have always been in the position of defending their cherished faith. Jude gave one of the first apologetic challenges: "Beloved, while I was making every effort to write you about our common salvation, I felt the necessity to write to you appealing that you contend earnestly for the faith which was once for all handed down to the saints" (Jude 3). Apologetics has consistently been an important element in the church, but each generation has adapted its approach to confront the unique challenges of its day. Today is no different.

The rapidly changing socioeconomic, political, racial, and religious landscape of today's world provides unique challenges. Yet we do not face these challenges in a vacuum. We are standing on the shoulders of giants. Fathers of the church such as Augustine, Aquinas, C.S. Lewis, and Francis Schaeffer have blazed a trail for us to follow. We must hold fast to that which is good, yet examine our approach with the utmost care (1 Thessalonians 5:21).

Regardless of the specific apologetic approach we adopt for ministry today, the bottom line is this: Apologetics for a new generation must be about winning people rather than winning arguments. The time of winning arguments and yet alienating people needs to come to an end. What good are the best arguments in the world without love? We do apologetics with a desire to be faithful to Scripture, yet we must always have an eye on advancing the kingdom of God.

This section will challenge you to consider the following questions: How do we most effectively do apologetics in this new generation? Is an objective approach to truth still important? How do we transform people's beliefs? You will enjoy Dan Kimball's opening chapter, "A Different Kind of Apologist."

Sean McDowell

A DIFFERENT KIND OF APOLOGIST

by Dan Kimball

A pologetics is desperately needed more than ever in our emerging culture. But I believe that a different kind of apologist may be needed.

I realize that some may disagree with me. I hear fairly often from some church leaders that emerging generations are not interested in apologetics: "In our postmodern world there isn't interest in rational explanations regarding spiritual issues." "We don't need logically presented defenses or offenses of the faith." These kinds of statements always confuse me. The reason is simple: In my dialogue and relationships with non-Christian and Christian young people for more than 18 years, I am not finding less interest in apologetics, but actually *more* interest. The more we are living in an increasingly post-Christian and pluralistic culture, the more we need apologetics because people are asking more and more questions. We desperately need to be ready to answer the tough questions of today's emerging generations.

This increased interest and need for apologetics in our emerging culture fits very nicely with one of the classical and well-known Bible passages on apologetics:

> But in your hearts set apart Christ as Lord. Always be prepared to give an answer to everyone who asks you to give the reason for the hope that you have. But do this with gentleness

and respect, keeping a clear conscience, so that those who speak maliciously against your good behavior in Christ may be ashamed of their slander (1 Peter 3:15-16 NIV).

Over the past couple of years I have heard apologists emphasize "gentleness and respect," which is an absolutely wonderful shift. Some Christians who are drawn to apologetics can have temperaments which may not always come out with gentleness and respect as they engage non-Christians. But this passage includes something else that, oddly, we don't hear much about. Yet it is critical for our discussion of apologetics for new generations.

People Can't Ask If They Don't Know Us

The passage in 1 Peter 3 says "Always be prepared to give an answer to everyone who asks you to give the reason for the hope that you have." Let me ask you, have you ever been standing on the street or in line at the supermarket and had a stranger walk up to you and say, "Excuse me. Can you tell me the reason for the hope that you have?"

That doesn't happen, because strangers do not generally walk up to people they don't know and ask questions like this. Strangers also don't know the other person, so they wouldn't be able to know if someone has hope or not. So how does someone know and trust Christians well enough to see the hope that they have and trust and respect them enough to ask them about it?

This is the biggest missing component in many of our approaches to apologetics today. It is one of the biggest shifts we are seeing with emerging generations. Apologetics is still needed today, but the apologist isn't necessarily trusted in our culture today. In the 1960s and 1970s, many younger people left the church because they (rightly) felt the church was often irrelevant. The critical questions that younger generations had at that time were not being answered. The music and various approaches to preaching and worship were becoming outdated and not speaking to new generations at that time. So when churches revamped their approaches to worship and preaching and developed clear answers for some of the questions people had, many people (even if they weren't Christian) became interested.

The culture still had a general respect for Christianity. So it was easier to communicate and also have a voice that folks would listen to. For those who grew up in a church but walked away, answers to their critical questions were extremely valuable. But today, Christians and the church aren't trusted like they were. Before, we were hoping to see people return to the church. Today, many have never been part of a church in the first place.

Times have changed. But the Spirit of God is still alive and active. People will always be created with questions about life, meaning, purpose, and God. Apologetics are still important today for new generations, but our approach must change.

Hanging Out with the Wrong People

In my early days as a Christian, I constantly read books on apologetics so I could share with my non-Christian friends about my newfound hope. My friends were concerned that I was following a religion and reading a book (the Bible) that they felt was written by primitive, ancient, and uneducated people. So this challenge kept me studying to respond to their concerns. The more I read and studied, the more my confidence in Christianity grew.

I eventually joined a large, wonderful church and made some friendships with others who also liked apologetics. We spent hours talking about theology, reasons why we could trust the Bible, and ways to respond to common objections such as the problem of evil. I bought almost every apologetics book available and attended many apologetics conferences. I loved having Christian friends whom I could talk to about apologetics, but something slowly dawned on me: I wasn't really talking to any non-Christians anymore about apologetics. I realized that I was hanging out all the time with Christians who loved discussing apologetics and the tough questions about the faith. But I wasn't spending time with the non-Christians who were asking these tough questions.

As I began exploring this further, I discovered that many people who like apologetics primarily socialize with other like-minded people. Certain temperaments and personalities cause some Christians to become more interested in apologetics than others, and they connect with each other. Having community with other Christians who share common interests such as apologetics is a wonderful thing. But I realized that my Christian friends and I weren't using apologetics to engage non-Christians. We were only talking with each other.

I discuss this in *They Like Jesus but Not the Church,* where I included this diagram, which lays out a typical pattern: The longer we are Christians, the less we socialize with non-Christians. We may work with non-Christians or have neighbors who are non-Christians. But the types of conversations we have and the trust that we build changes dramatically when we actually befriend and socialize with those outside the faith.

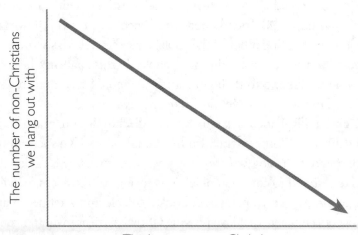

The longer we are Christians

The danger is that we don't do this on purpose. It happens unintentionally. But because we have limited time and we enjoy hanging out with others who think like us, we can remove ourselves from the very ones we are sent by Jesus to be salt and light to (Matthew 5). As the Spirit molds us to be more like Jesus, the majority of people who benefit from our growth are already Christians. We are salt and light to each other, not to the world. The more skilled in apologetics we get, the fewer people we know who actually need it.

You may resist hearing this, and I hope I am wrong about you. But let me ask you a question or three:

1. Think about discussions you have had about apologetics with people in the past six months. How many have been with Christians, and how many have been with those who aren't Christians yet?

Let me make this more direct and personal:

2. Who are your non-Christian friends?

When was the last time you went out to a movie or dinner or simply hung out with a non-Christian? If people are to trust us in order to ask us for the hope we have, we must spend time with them and build relationships. The typical answers I get from Christians quite honestly scare me. Again, I hope I am wrong about you. Do you intentionally place yourself in situations or groups where you will be likely to meet new people? For me, music often provides an open door. So whether I'm with the manager of a coffee house I frequent or the members of local bands, I try to have the mind-set of a missionary and meet new people. This sounds so elementary and I almost feel silly having to type this out. But this leads to a deeper question:

3. Who are you praying for regularly that is not a Christian?

Our prayers represent our hearts. What we pray for shows us what we are thinking about and valuing. When the unsaved become more than faces in the crowd, when they include people we know and care for, we can't help but pray for them. And we must remember: We can be prepared with apologetic arguments, but the Spirit does the persuading. Are you regularly praying for some non-Christian friends?

Again, I feel almost embarrassed asking this. But when I started realizing that I had fallen into this trap, I wondered if I was alone. As I began asking other Christians about this, many seemed to be like me. I even asked an author of apologetics books to tell me about his recent conversations with non-Christians that included apologetics. But he couldn't remember any recent examples. He was talking only to Christians! This isn't bad, but it raises an important question: How do we know the questions emerging generations outside the church are asking if we are only talking with Christians?

I recently talked with a person who teaches apologetics to young people. As we talked, he shared how interested youth are in apologetics (and I fully agree). I asked about the types of questions he is hearing, and I was surprised that his experience seemed quite different from mine. I was working with non-Christian youth at that time, but he was speaking primarily with Christian youth at Christian schools and youth groups. Nothing is wrong with teaching Christian youth how to have confidence in their faith through apologetics. This is an important task we need to be doing today in our churches. But if we are focusing our energy and time listening mainly to Christians, how do we know what the questions non-Christian youth or young adults have? This brings me to my next point.

Providing Answers Before Listening to Questions

The effective apologist to emerging generations will be a good listener. Most of us have been good talkers. We Christians often do the talking and expect others to listen. But in our emerging culture, effective communication involves dialogue. Being quiet and asking questions may not be easy for some folks, but those are critical skills we need to develop in order to reach new generations.

A 20-year-old Hindu became friends with someone in our church. Eventually she began coming to our worship gatherings. I got to meet with her at a coffee house, and because I was sincerely curious, I politely asked her some questions. How did she become a Hindu? What is Hinduism to her? What does she find most beneficial in her life about it? She eagerly told me stories that helped me understand her journey and her specific beliefs. As much as I wanted to, I didn't interrupt her or jump in to correct her when I felt she was saying things that may have been inconsistent. I didn't interrupt and tell her that there cannot be hundreds of gods, that there is only one true God. I simply asked questions and listened carefully.

Eventually, she asked me about the differences between Christianity and Hinduism. I gently and respectfully tried to compare her story and what she said with the story of Jesus and the narrative of the Bible. But I didn't try to discredit her beliefs or show why what I believed was true. She asked me about the origins of Christianity, and I was able to draw a timeline on a napkin that included creation, the Garden of Eden, and the fall. I explained that people eventually began worshipping other gods or goddesses, not the original one God. I then walked her through a basic world religions timeline I had memorized and explained where Hinduism fit in that timeline. It truly was a dialogue, as I would stop and see if she had any input or comments.

I didn't show her why I felt Hinduism was wrong; rather, I let our discussion speak for itself. The differences between Christianity and Hinduism became obvious. A few weeks later, she told me in a worship gathering that she had left Hinduism and chosen to follow Jesus. My talk with her was not the turning point. She had many conversations with other Christian friends in our church. They knew her beliefs, loved her, invited her into community, and lived out the hope they have. She could see it and experience it, and eventually she wanted to know the reason for the hope in her friends. I definitely needed to be ready with apologetics when I met with her. But the reason she even met with me was that we built trust first. Trust was built with some of her Christian friends. Trust was built during conversations I had with her when she came to our worship gatherings. Eventually, this trust led to her being open to dialogue specifically about her Hindu faith and to ask questions. First she was valued as a person and listened to, and then came the questions about the hope we have. Let me ask you a few questions about this:

1. On a scale of 1 to 10, how would you rate yourself as a listener in conversations about faith?

2. What are some of the questions you have been asked as a result of building trust and listening? Would anyone have asked those questions if you didn't build trust and listen first?

Stockpiling Ammunition or Building Trust

I recently heard of someone who was taking church groups on the street to walk up to total strangers and strike up conversations and then use apologetics with them. I respect the passion to reach lost people, but I was saddened by the methodology. The leader chose this area because it was highly populated with homosexuals. From my perspective, this is almost the opposite of the methodology that is effective with new generations. We may have our apologetics gun loaded, but we haven't built trust. We haven't gained a voice in their lives, so they don't trust us enough to listen to us. Walking up to total strangers and asking them questions about very personal things immediately puts them on the defense. The discussion begins in a semi-confrontational way. This reinforces some of the stereotypes of Christians we need to break. Non-Christians are often open to discussing personal beliefs about religion and worldviews, but this normally occurs in the context of trust and friendship.

I recently met a guy in his twenties who was working at a coffee house. I did my usual thing: I selected one place to frequent and eventually got to know those who work there. We eventually started talking about all kinds of things, mainly music at first. Eventually I told him I was a pastor at a church and began asking his opinion on things. I asked about his impressions of church and Christianity. I shared that I knew about Christians' bad reputation and that I wanted to know how he felt about that. This wasn't the first thing we talked about, and we had begun to build a friendship, so he was happy to talk to me about this. One of his main issues was that the Christians he met knew nothing about other religions, but they would tell him he should be a Christian. His concern was that Christians were naive about anything but what they believed, and he didn't respect that.

As I listened, I didn't try to butt in and comment when he would say something I disagreed with. Instead, I listened, asked clarifying questions, took notes, and thanked him for each opinion. I asked him what he believed and why he believed what he did. And then the inevitable happened—he asked me what I believed.

Knowing his beliefs, I was able to construct an apologetic that catered to his story and specific points of connection. As with so many people, the issue of pluralism and world religions was a major point of tension that he felt Christians are blind about. Eventually our conversation moved to the resurrection of Jesus, which he saw as a myth. I used the classical Josh McDowell resurrection apologetics, explaining various theories of the stolen body and why they fell apart upon scrutiny. I shared about the guards at the tomb and how they would defend the sealed tomb. I was ready (thanks to Josh McDowell), and my friend was absolutely fascinated by that. I could tell he had never heard this before, and as we ended our time together, he thanked me. I didn't press him for a response.

The following week I went back to the coffee house, and he told me that he now believed in the resurrection. He had been totally unaware that there are actually good reasons to believe it is true. Over the weekend he got a copy of the Bible to read the resurrection story and had no idea it was repeated in each of the Gospels. This is why I am convinced that regardless of how postmodern emerging generations may be, they receive apologetic arguments when trust is built. Of course, it is the Holy Spirit who does the work in someone's heart—not clever arguments. But God still uses apologetics in our emerging culture.

Consider these questions:

1. When you are studying apologetics, does your heart break in compassion for the people you are preparing to talk to? Or are you stockpiling ammunition to show people they are wrong?

2. When you have used apologetics with those who aren't Christians yet, do you find your tone being humble, broken, and compassionate, or is your tone argumentative and perhaps even arrogant (although you would not like to admit that)?

Critical Apologetics Issues

I know that most apologists are not arrogant, ammunition firing, non-listening people who don't have any non-Christian friends and only talk to other Christians. But at the same time, a little hyperbole may raise up some ugly truth we perhaps need to admit. As I shared, I know I have been guilty of these very things. We must all examine ourselves and be brutally honest about it. Too much is at stake not to.

As statistics are showing, we are not doing a very good job of reaching new generations. Our reputation is suffering. But at the same time, I have so much optimism and hope. Apologetics is a *critical* factor in the evangelism of new generations. That is why I was thrilled to be part of this book.

If you are a leader in a church, I hope you are creating a natural culture in your church of teaching apologetics and training people how to respond to others when asked for the hope that they have. But again, *how* we train them to respond is just as important as the answers themselves. The attitudes and tone of voice we use as we teach reveal what we truly feel about those who aren't Christians and their beliefs. Our hearts should be broken thinking of people who have developed false worldviews or religious beliefs and don't know Jesus yet. How we teach people in our church to be "listeners" and build friendships is critical. Here are some of the key things we must be ready to answer today:

- *The inspiration and trustworthiness of the Bible.* Everything comes back to why we trust the Bible and what it says about human sexuality, world religions...everything. Why the Bible is more credible than other world religious writings is critical.

- *Who is Jesus?* Emerging generations are open to talking about Jesus but for the most part, they have an impression that He is more like Gandhi than a divine Savior. This gives us a wonderful opportunity to share why Jesus is unique and to provide an apologetic for His resurrection.

- *Human sexuality.* We need to be well-versed in why we believe what we do about the covenant of marriage between a man and woman, about human sexuality, and about sexual ethics in general.

- *World religions.* We must have an adequate understanding of the development and teachings of world religions. I don't meet many younger people who are hard-core Buddhists, but many are empathetic to Buddhist teachings. Many pick and choose from different faiths. They are often surprised to see that many religions are mutually exclusive.

The Most Important Apologetic

As I close this chapter, I want to remind us that the ultimate apologetic is really Jesus in us. Are our lives demonstrating the fruit of the Spirit (Galatians 5), such as gentleness, kindness, patience, and love? Are we being salt and light with our attitudes and actions toward people? Are our conversations filled with grace and seasoned with salt (Colossians 4:6)? Do our lives show that we are paying attention to the things Jesus would, including the marginalized, the oppressed, and the poor? People watch and listen. If they trust the messenger, perhaps they will be more open to listen.

We can have all the answers ready to give people who ask, but are they asking us? If not, perhaps we have not yet built the trust and relationship and respect that lead them to ask us for the hope we have. Maybe that's where we need to start—with our hearts and lives. If we will, I can almost guarantee that others will ask us for the hope we have.

May God use us together on the mission of Jesus as we are wise as serpents but as innocent as doves. May God use our minds and hearts to bring the reason for the hope we have to others. And may God put others in our lives who will ask for the hope as they watch us live it out.

> **Dan Kimball** is the author of several books, including *They Like Jesus but Not the Church,* and a member of the staff of Vintage Faith Church in Santa Cruz, California.

TRUTH NEVER GETS OLD

by Brett Kunkle

O n October 17, 2005, the world changed. At approximately 5:03 p.m. eastern standard time, in the inaugural episode of *The Colbert Report,* Stephen Colbert introduced the world to a new word: "truthiness." Colbert explained:

> It used to be, everyone was entitled to their own opinion, but not their own facts. But that's not the case anymore. Facts matter not at all. Perception is everything...Truthiness is "What I say is right, and [nothing] anyone else says could possibly be true." It's not only that I *feel* it to be true, but that *I* feel it to be true.[1]

Then came the recognition all words dream of, the Oscar of awards for words. The American Dialect Society chose "truthiness" as the 2005 Word of the Year.[2] The Merriam-Webster dictionary followed, naming truthiness its 2006 Word of the Year. Never had a single linguistic utterance captured consecutive Word of the Year awards.

It was a sign of the times.

Relativism Is Alive and Well

Of course, *The Colbert Report* is satire, and we laugh at Colbert's ridiculously extreme statements. But the funniest part is this—his outlandish comments often reflect something that is actually happening in our culture. Truthiness captures the spirit of the age: relativism.

Relativism has a multitude of expressions and is alive and well in our culture.

According to George Barna, more than nine out of ten Christian students affirms moral relativism.[3] Some church leaders point to this trend as a sign of the culture's corrosive impact on our youth, and they sound a call to arms. But new voices in the church are telling a different story.

Emergent Village leader Brian McLaren claims that except for a few drunk college students, no one embraces the brand of relativism some Christian leaders fear.[4] McLaren declares, "Arguments that pit absolutism versus relativism, and objectivism versus subjectivism, prove meaningless or absurd to postmodern people."[5]

So which is it? Should we train a new generation to defend the idea of truth against the threat of relativism, or is this an outdated strategy? Answering this question is critical. The gospel is never heard in isolation. Particular cultural ideas either help or hinder its spread. If we misdiagnose the problem, our prescription will likely be wrong too, and the gospel will suffer.

First, let me be clear on what I mean by relativism. Atheist philosopher Friedrich Nietzsche put it this way: "You have your way. I have my way. As for the right way, the correct way, and the only way, it does not exist."[6] According to Nietzsche then, who determines what is true? We do. Truth is relative to either the group or the individual. It's up to us. We simply do our own thing.

A more tame version of this kind of relativism is flourishing in the emerging generation. In 2005, sociologist Christian Smith released the main findings of the largest and most thorough study of teenagers and religion ever undertaken. His book is titled *Soul Searching: The Religious and Spiritual Lives of American Teenagers*. The findings were the result of four years of in-depth research by the National Study of Youth and Religion.

Smith and his team of researchers found that in matters of religion, teens were profoundly relativistic. When asked about religion and truth, fewer than one-third said they believed only one religion was true.[7] By contrast, 60 percent were convinced that many religions may be true. Christian students fared no better. Of conservative Protestant teens, only 46 percent believed that one religion was true, a belief shared by one in four mainline Protestant teens.[8] Smith concludes, American teenagers "lean toward an open and inclusive religious pluralism on the matter of religions' truth claims."[9]

Smith and his researchers found religious relativism went virtually unquestioned among teenagers. It's part of the air they breathe.

> American youth, like American adults, are nearly without exception profoundly individualistic…The typical bywords… are "Who am I to judge?" "If that's what they choose, whatever," "Each person decides for himself," and "If it works for them, fine"…Some version of this individualistic subjectivism and relativism is the dominant, assumed viewpoint about religion among most contemporary U.S. adolescents.[10]

Clearly, relativism rules not only among teens but also in culture in general. And conservative Christians are not the only ones sounding the alarm.

In 2005, Cardinal Joseph Ratzinger, now Pope Benedict XVI, warned Catholics of the "dictatorship of relativism that does not recognize anything as definitive."[11] In 2008, Benedict spoke to more than 140,000 people at the Catholic youth festival in Sydney, Australia. He warned that relativism does not lead "to genuine freedom, but to moral or intellectual confusion."[12]

When "truthiness" received Merriam-Webster's 2006 Word of the Year award, president John Morse explained why: "We're at a point where what constitutes truth is a question on a lot of people's minds, and truth has become up for grabs."[13]

Other nonreligious voices have weighed in. Prominent secular psychologists Edmund Bourne and Lorna Garano note that moral relativism has come to dominate modern life: "There is no shared, consistent, socially-agreed-upon set of values and standards for people to live by." They add that this is a major cause of anxiety among Americans.[14]

My own experience confirms our culture's relativistic impulse. My work gives me the opportunity to speak with thousands of Christian and non-Christian students and adults across the country every year. When I speak to a typical group of teenagers, I can count on the fact that the majority of them will be religious pluralists and moral relativists, a suspicion that's confirmed almost every time I offer a "truth test" (you'll see it later in this chapter). The only exceptions are those students who have had training in apologetics.

Recently, I spoke at a large convention in Southern California. As I addressed a mix of lay leaders and vocational pastors about the challenge of relativism, I realized that many of them were relativists. One young youth worker argued that Christians should not impose their views about abortion on those who don't share them. They are merely *our* Christian beliefs, true for us, but not for everyone. A Sunday school teacher pointed to the religious diversity in our culture and warned about claiming there is only one true religion. I scrapped my prepared talk and instead addressed the challenge of relativism coming even from these Christian leaders.

Please hear me. I'm not saying every American is a relativist. I am not saying students everywhere embrace relativism. However, it's clear that Americans are swimming in a sea of relativism. And the cultural tide continues to erode our confidence in truth.

So how should the church respond? Some emerging church leaders like Tony Jones, author of *Postmodern Youth Ministry,* recognize the rampant relativism in culture. According to Jones, however, warnings about relativism are a Christian scare tactic to combat postmodernism, or worse, a ploy by Christian leaders to raise lots of money and pack arenas with students using fear-based rhetoric.[15] According to Jones, resistance is futile and unnecessary. We should embrace relativism, not fight it.[16]

Brian McLaren goes further, prescribing relativism as an evil but necessary short-term postmodern cure for the church's absolutist hangover from modernity. According to McLaren, "Relativism is like a chemotherapy introduced to stop the spread of holocaust…Modern

Christians often see the danger of relativism and seek to retreat into absolutism."[17] McLaren suggests we see the short-term value of relativism as a healing agent rather than a hostile enemy. But if taken too long or in too large a dose, the cure can kill the patient.

Relativism—Bad Medicine

Make no mistake. If we embrace relativism, it will undermine the Christian convictions of our youth. Ideas have consequences. Relativistic ideas about truth strip away the transformative power of the gospel in young lives in at least three ways.

Relativism Diminishes Sin

If Nietzsche's extreme brand of relativism is true, there are no objective moral facts that hold true for everyone. If morality is subjective, moral choices are mere preferences. And if right and wrong are simply matters of taste, sin evaporates, neutering the gospel.

"Gospel" (*euangelion* in Greek) literally means "good news." But *this* good news implies some very bad news. And here Scripture is very clear. Sin is the disease that is cured by the good news Jesus brings. However, if radical relativism is true, then there is no moral law, no sin, and no good news. The gospel is neutralized, and Christianity loses its voice. C.S. Lewis points out, "It is after you have realized that there is a Moral Law and a Power behind that law, and that you have broken the law and put yourself wrong with that Power—it is after this and not a moment sooner, that Christianity begins to talk."[18] Christianity has nothing to say to young people if they are convinced Nietzsche's relativism is true because once sin disappears, grace disappears with it.

The impact this has on students is unmistakable. In *Soul Searching,* Christian Smith found students seesawing between their commonsense moral intuitions and a morally relativistic impulse that "forswears judging any ideas." The vocabulary students commonly use tells the story. According to Smith, "certain traditional religious languages and vocabularies of commitment, duty, faithfulness, obedience, calling, obligation, accountability, and ties to the past are nearly completely absent from the discourse of U.S. teenagers."[19] The reason? Such words only make sense if objective moral truths exist.

Test your own students. Ask them some version of this question: What does it mean to be a Christian? In response, you'll hear talk about relationship with God or following Jesus, important concepts to be sure. Take note, however, of what is missing:

- repentance of sins (Luke 5:32; Acts 3:19)

- atonement for sins (Romans 3:25)

- forgiveness (John 16:8)

- freedom from God's wrath (John 3:36; Romans 5:9)

- justification before God (Romans 5:16)

- reconciliation with God (2 Corinthians 5:18-20)

Aren't these ideas essential to the gospel? Yet these are the very things that relativism ultimately renders meaningless, stripping the gospel of its transformative truth and power.

Relativism Erodes Moral Conviction

After a few short years, our young people leave the safety of Christian homes, churches, and youth groups and forge ahead on their own. What will keep them following Jesus when they are far removed from friends, parents, and church leaders?

Study after study demonstrates the moral perils facing young people. And Christians are not immune. In his book *Forbidden Fruit: Sex and Religion in the Lives of American Teenagers,* sociologist Mark Regnerus opens our eyes to evangelical teen sexuality. He finds that Christian youth engage in premarital sex almost as much as their non-evangelical counterparts.

When your student finds herself alone in a dorm room with her boyfriend, what factors influence her decision to give in or to send him packing? Her moral convictions play a central role. Sheer relativism says that her moral standards turn out to be nothing more than preferences. And preferences can change in a heartbeat, especially when the heart is beating overtime. If she begins to suspect that objective moral truth doesn't exist, her moral convictions will quickly wither.

Relativism Makes Religion Irrelevant

Some church leaders are convinced that our nation's youth are irretrievably postmodern. As we saw earlier, writers like Brian McLaren think a modernist approach to truth is ineffective with postmoderns who use a different vocabulary for truth. But McClaren qualifies this by explaining that today's postmodernism is different from that of Nietzsche.

Listen carefully and you'll notice young people assume, in most areas of everyday life, that truth is objective. No one is postmodern, for example, when balancing a checkbook, reading the directions on a medicine bottle, or simply walking across the street.

Gregory Koukl, coauthor of *Relativism: Feet Firmly Planted in Mid-Air,* puts it this way:

> Everyone is already deeply convinced of the truth, even when he denies it. True, our culture is driven by a postmodern impulse, but deep down each of us is a common-sense realist. Those who are not are either dead, in an institution, or sleeping in cardboard boxes under the freeway.[20]

But we are inconsistent here. Most Westerners function with a worldview split in two, what sociologists refer to as the public/private split.[21] In the public sphere, we operate in the realm of rationality, knowledge, facts, and objective truth. Doctors, scientists, corporations, and the state conduct their matters here. In the private sphere are institutions—like family and church—driven by personal preference, opinion, and subjective (relative) truth. Matters of religion and morality are confined to this realm. Accordingly, "Religion is not considered an objective truth to which we submit, but only a matter of personal taste which we choose."[22]

Here's the devastating result. This split effectively severs Christ from our public life—where we live most of our lives—and consigns Him to our private prayer closets. Let me illustrate.

Do college students spend four years of study researching family traditions to find the true traditions that should be practiced in society? Of course not. Those "truths" are relative, a matter of personal preference. Rather, those students will study science, medicine, and technology to discover facts that have implications for all areas of life.

Christian Smith discovered what happens when religion is relativized and relegated to the realm of personal preference and mere opinion: Religion becomes compartmentalized in the daily experience of most American teenagers. Thus, "religion simply doesn't seem consequential enough to most teenagers to pay close attention to and get right." As a result, American teenagers are "*incredibly inarticulate* about their faith, their religious beliefs and practices, and its meaning or place in their lives."[23] In a word, religion becomes irrelevant, and when this happens, Christ becomes irrelevant too.

Might this explain why youth in our churches are often passionless about Christ? He has been severed from the very things that occupy most of their lives. How can they be passionate about Christ when He seem so inconsequential? Might this also explain why many Christian young people are double minded? Morality is mere preference, and preferences come in all shapes and sizes. That's why you'll see students who, on their Facebook or MySpace profiles, identify themselves as Christians who love Jesus and yet down the page post sexually suggestive pictures, risqué images, and vulgarities. Why? Because their relationship with Jesus is only part of their life—the private part.

I recently reconnected with a student from my Colorado youth ministry days on Facebook. As I scanned his profile, I noticed he identified himself as a conservative Christian and included a word about God and prayer in the Quotes section. However, his Status Update essentially read, "F——— those guys who stole my backpack today. I hope you get the s—— kicked out of you." Of course, we all have bad days and can identify with the temptation to let a few choice words fly. But I am struck by the regular inconsistencies I see on the social networking profiles of Christian youth where Christ and crudeness coexist seamlessly.

For many of our students, Christianity is trapped in the realm of relativism. This prevents Christ from informing every area of their lives. For them, relativism has made Christ irrelevant to the rest of life.

A final note about relativism's impact. Notice I did not say that young people who embrace relativism will kill someone soon. I did not say they'll become nihilists who don't care about anyone or anything. And I didn't say that if they become relativists, they're on a "slippery slope to Hell."[24] Relativism's impact is often quiet and subtle. On the broad spectrum of relativistic belief, students range from one end to the other. Rather than bringing instant destruction, relativism slowly erodes a young person's religious and moral convictions.

Are your students relativistic in religion and morality? To find out, test them. First be sure they are clear on the difference between subjective truth and objective truth. Give them an analogy to clarify the distinction. Have them consider, for example, the difference between ice cream and insulin. Is there a single flavor of ice cream that is the right flavor? Do we fault others for choosing chocolate over vanilla? Of course not. Ice cream preferences are subjective truths—true for some, but not for others.

Contrast ice cream with insulin. If your doctor diagnoses you with diabetes, does he ask your preference in medicine? Again, of course not. You want the right medicine, and this has nothing to do with your personal preferences. Even if you sincerely believed ice cream could control diabetes, the facts would not change.[25] Regardless of preferences, diabetics still need insulin, not ice cream.

Now for the test. Read the following statements (or come up with your own) and ask students to identify the statement as subjective truth or objective truth:

TRUTH TEST:
Ice Cream (Subjective) or Insulin (Objective)?

	Objective	Subjective
1. That shirt is red.	☐	☐
2. Red is the most beautiful color.	☐	☐
3. 2 + 2 = 4	☐	☐
4. Tropical island vacations are the best kind.	☐	☐
5. Atoms consists of protons, neutrons, and electrons.	☐	☐
6. Brett can bench press 350 pounds. (Okay, maybe it's false, but it's still objective.)	☐	☐
7. God exists.	☐	☐
8. Jesus is the only way to God, even for Jews.	☐	☐
9. Premarital sex is immoral.	☐	☐
10. Elective abortions are immoral.	☐	☐

The first five are fairly simple. Number 6 might trip up a few students because it's false even though it is an objective claim. Remember, objective claims are *either* true or false, while subjective claims are *neither* true nor false. Students infected with relativism will either hedge or flatly affirm relativism on statements 7 through 10. Then you'll know if your student is a relativist in matters of religion and morality.

Bringing Truth to Life

Relativism is flourishing in culture, infecting the emerging generation. Its consequences are serious, robbing Christianity of its relevance for our young people. It's time for decisive action. This means creating cultures of truth in our homes, our churches, our youth ministries, and our Christian schools. Resisting relativism's corrosive influence is not enough. We need to empower students to be agents of transformation to their generation. But how do we make truth a part of their daily experience? How do we teach them to bring Christ into all areas of life?

Elevate Your Expectations

In academics and athletics, we have high expectations for our kids. But when it comes to theological training, we drop the bar so low, most of our kids learn nothing about essential Christian doctrines. Don't believe me? Ask them about the basics. See if they can move beyond Christian clichés and offer anything of substance. Then ask them *why* they believe. Can they offer good reasons for their convictions?

Recall Christian Smith's finding that students are "incredibly inarticulate" about religion. To make the point, Smith offers a typical example: a 15-year-old Protestant Christian girl who "attends two church services every Sunday, Sunday school, church youth group, and Wednesday-night Bible study." When asked about her own personal religious beliefs, though, here is all she could muster:

> I think that you should just, if you're gonna do something wrong then you should always ask for forgiveness and he's gonna forgive you no matter what, 'cause he gave up his only son to take all the sins for you, so.[26]

Smith notes that generally teens are articulate in areas where they are effectively educated. He sensed, though, that his interview was the first time any adult had ever asked this teenager what she believed and how it mattered in her life.[27] We can—and must—raise the bar.

Ground Truth in Reality

Fortunately, truth has a powerful ally: reality. If we're going to recapture young minds for truth, they must first understand the nature of truth. And reality is central to that understanding.

When "truthiness" won Word of the Year in 2005, linguist Michael Adams explained, "The national argument right now is, one, who's got the truth and, two, who's got the facts. Until we can manage to get the two of them back together again, we're not going to make much progress."[28] Adams was spot on. Facts, not personal preferences, make statements true. Beliefs are only true if they fit the facts.[29]

Return to the truth test. What makes statements 7 through 10 objective truths? Reality. They correspond to the way the world really is. Our young people need to be confident that our religious and moral claims are more than mere opinion. "God exists" is an objective claim about the world "out there." It is either true or false. Moral truths are not merely preferences. Real moral laws are grounded in reality and inform our behavior.

Is anything more sobering in life than reality? When our beliefs about the world are false, people get hurt. When relativistic beliefs lead the emerging generation astray, they get injured. But hope finds its beginning in reality. Youth can count on reality when their beliefs are true. And because Christ is true and central to all reality, the emerging generation has the ultimate reason for hope. This is the reality we must constantly bring them back to.

Ask "Why" Before They Do

Don't fear tough questions from your students. Rather, raise these questions before they do and join them in the search. This approach has three advantages.

First, it creates a safe environment for students to express doubt and grapple with tough questions. They don't need to be ashamed of their doubts. Instead, create a safe place for them to explore their doubts and questions honestly with friends and leaders who love them. They won't get that from hostile atheist professors a thousand miles from home.

Second, it creates opportunities for humility—on our part. Young people will ask questions we can't answer. It's okay that you're not omniscient. In fact, here are three words you can practice for those situations: "I don't know." Young people find such honesty refreshing. And they're more likely to seek answers, with you as their companion in the search.

Third, it creates opportunities for greater faith. Doubts that are answered and overturned will strengthen your student's trust in the truth and will fortify confidence in their convictions.

Integrate Character with Truth

Teaching truth does not mean spouting cold facts or sterile propositions. Rather, the goal is transformation of mind *and* heart, resulting in love of God and neighbor (Matthew 22:37-39). First Peter 3:15 tells us to be ready to make a defense for our hope in Christ. But don't miss the context. Peter says that first we must sanctify Christ as Lord in our hearts. When we are properly related to Christ, our defense becomes gentle and respectful. Therefore, character and truth go together. I have two suggestions in this regard.

First, learn to defend the truth without being defensive. Defensiveness suggests a lack of confidence. But why should we lack confidence if we have the truth? And if we don't have the truth, wouldn't we want to know? If Christianity is true, then every objection and argument raised against it will be flawed somewhere. Quiet confidence should replace defensiveness.

Second, model confidence in the truth even though absolute certainty evades you, as it often will. Even when we have good reasons for our convictions, our own grasp of truth is fallible. Omniscience is for God, not us. Show humble confidence to our youth based on the good reasons we have, not arrogant certainty that goes beyond our evidence.

Create Opportunities to Engage the World with Truth

Is training in the truth confined behind the walls of the church? It shouldn't be. We can bring the truth to life when we connect students with the real world. Are you teaching your students about world religions? Great. Have classroom instruction, but don't stop there. Bring in your Mormon neighbor or LDS missionaries so students can ask them questions. Take a tour of the local Buddhist temple or engage your friendly neighborhood Hindu.

Are you teaching on evolution? Don't confine it to the classroom. Instead, find a science museum in your area and ask the curator for a tour and Q and A session. Let the classroom teaching come to life as students engage a real-life evolutionist with the truth.

It's time to get our youth out of the church and into the world. For the past few years, I've helped students interact with atheists in Berkeley and Mormons in Utah.[30] We have created hundreds of real-time, real-life experiences allowing them to engage real people with the truth. Nothing I do has been more effective to train students. Every time they come back more passionate about the truth.

An Old Word About Truth

Above all, we must embody the truth for our young people. Life with Christ is more than a set of true propositions. Note Blaise Pascal, a Christian sage from the past:

> Men despise religion. They hate it and are afraid it may be true. The cure for this is first to show that religion is not contrary to reason, but worthy of reverence and respect. Next make it attractive, make good men wish it were true, and then show that it is. Worthy of reverence because it really understands human nature. Attractive because it promises true good.[31]

When we contend for the truth of Christianity (Jude 3), we show it's not contrary to reason. If our lives also embody Christ's truth, we make it attractive. In so doing, we become full of grace *and* truth, like Jesus (John 1:14).

That kind of truth never gets old.

Brett Kunkle is the student impact director at Stand to Reason and a regular guest host of Stand to Reason's weekly radio show.

AN INTERVIEW WITH LEE STROBEL

Sean McDowell: How important is apologetics training today?

Lee Strobel: We're seeing a resurgence of interest in apologetics, especially among young people. The reason is that we have a wealth right now of books by atheists and skeptics attacking the Christian faith. This has thrown a lot of Christians on their heels because they don't know how to respond to this stuff. And it has caused a lot of spiritual seekers to look beyond Christianity for answers.

Sean: What are some effective ways to use apologetics today?

Lee: Stories are very important because Jesus told stories, and people respond to them. Kids love film in a way that I never did growing up. The other thing that is critically important is conversational apologetics. We can no longer sit down and pin up to the wall 50 reasons to believe. It's more about sharing why you believe, asking what questions people have, and genuinely listening. Doing apologetics through relationships, with conversation and mutual respect, bears much more fruit these days than when people sense that we are preaching at them. Apologetics knocks down objections people have and gives them an opportunity to come face-to-face with God.

Sean: How important is the character of the apologist?

Lee: Twenty-first-century apologetics must come from a person whose life is authentically changed by Christ and is living consistently with the faith. However, I've met an awful lot of nice Mormons and Muslims! This is not a niceness contest. People have to know that they are in trouble with a holy God and that their wrongdoing has separated them from God. The only one who can bridge that gap is Jesus, who lived a perfect life and died as a substitute to pay for our sins so we can receive forgiveness and eternal life. I do not think Christianity advances if people just come to the conclusion that we are nicer than other people. Ravi Zacharias had a great line. He said that Jesus did not come to make bad people good. He came to make dead people live.

Sean: What trends do you see in how apologetics is being done in the church today?

Lee: More churches are training and equipping people to defend their beliefs. There is tremendous growth in quality apologetics resources. I'm also seeing more and more debates in the United States, and I have mixed feelings about them. I think debates in one sense stimulate discussion. On the negative side, they tend to polarize people in the wrong camps. The biggest trend that I am seeing in evangelism in the world right now is what I call "seeker small groups." These are small groups of nonbelievers meeting with a Christian or Christian couple over a period of time, investigating spiritual issues.

Sean: What advice would you give to pastors and youth pastors?

Lee: Take advantage of the good resources that are available. And do not set yourself up on a pedestal as if you had all the answers. It's okay to say, "That's a good question. I've wrestled with that too. You know what, let's check it out together." Also, pastors themselves need to engage in spiritual conversations with nonbelievers and get into the trenches more, where they're forced personally to confront a lot of the issues that people are raising. When you are in the trenches, you experience what it is like to have a nonbeliever raise some thorny questions. If you are not experienced in that, chances are that you are not going to inspire your people to do it either. The pastor sets the standard.

> **Lee Strobel** is a *New York Times* bestselling author of nearly 20 books, including *The Case for Christ*.

A FRESH APOLOGETIC:
RELATIONSHIPS THAT TRANSFORM

by Josh McDowell

Brace yourself.

Some of the things I will share with you in this chapter may sound strange to you. They may sound contrary to the way you were raised, the way you think, the way you perceive the gospel of Jesus Christ, and the way you typically relate to truth itself. Some of my words may surprise you and maybe even shock you. But though such a response may be unavoidable, I am not trying to provoke such a reaction. Instead, I want to present you with one of the most important discoveries of my life in the hope that it will transform your life and the lives of many people around you—and even the church itself.

Not long ago, I visited a large church in the Midwest to speak to pastors, parents, and many others over the course of a weekend. The church's new facility, surrounded by cornfields and wooded areas, dominated the rural landscape. As I approached the entrance, I couldn't help noticing the enormous banner hung across the front of the church building. The banner announced, in large, bold letters, "We preach the truth—and the truth only!" I felt a wave of sadness wash over me. If that sign truly reflects the attitude of that church, they might as well close their doors now, for they will surely fail.

The Whole Truth

"But, Josh, how can you say that? You've dedicated a lifetime of energy and passion to telling the world the truth! How can you say that a church that preaches 'the truth—and the truth only' is doomed to failure?" This is the reaction I received from the pastor of that church, but by the end of the weekend, he indicated that his attitude had begun to change. I hope and pray that the same thing will happen in all of us for the sake of our children and grandchildren and for all those in our families, churches, and communities who haven't yet experienced new life in Christ.

We live in a culture that is generally uninterested in the truth of the gospel, partly because they are thoroughly unimpressed by those who proclaim it. A flurry of recent studies and books with titles like *unChristian: What a New Generation Really Thinks About Christianity* and *They Like Jesus but Not the Church,* say strikingly similar things.[1] For example, in 1996, 15 percent of people outside the church had extremely bad impressions of Christians and Christianity; by 2007 that number had ballooned to 38 percent.[2] One in four say they believe that that modern-day Christianity is no longer like Jesus.[3]

More specifically, when non-Christians and nonchurchgoers give their opinions about those of us who are committed to the truth of the gospel...

- 87 percent believe the church is judgmental.

- 85 percent believe the church is hypocritical.

- 86 percent believe Christianity is phony and unreal.[4]

So you see, we can preach the truth—and only the truth—from now until Jesus returns and meet with utter disinterest from those around us because they are not looking for what they see in us. They don't want the truth from us. And that's directly related to our failure to grasp, live, and communicate "the whole counsel of God" (Acts 20:27 ESV).

What Engenders Belief

When the pastor of that church asked me how I could take issue with his church's boast about preaching "the truth—and the truth only," I explained to him that it was not the proclamation of truth that turned the world upside down in the apostles' day or in more recent times.

This is an issue I wrestled with for roughly 15 years, and the light finally came on about 9 years ago: What engenders belief in a young person? In any person, for that matter? In other words, what will cause your children, grandchildren, students, neighbors, friends, and family members to want to hear the truth, know Jesus, follow the Scriptures, and live out the values you yourself treasure?

I think I can answer that question now in a single word: relationships.

You may counter by saying, "No, Josh, it's the Holy Spirit who engenders faith in a person." Yes, of course that is true. But what does the Holy Spirit use? He doesn't work in a vacuum. More than anything else, He will use relationships to stimulate belief.

King David said, "I am always aware of your unfailing love" (Psalm 26:3 NLT). Notice he didn't say once in a while or even a couple times a week. He said, "I am *always* aware of your unfailing love." What did that do to David? What did such an awareness produce in him? The rest of the verse provides the answer: "And I have lived according to your truth." David clearly connected his constant awareness of God's love with living according to the truth.

He does much the same thing in Psalm 86, when he prays, "Teach me your ways, O LORD, that I may live according to your truth" (Psalm 86:11 NLT). That is a prayer that certainly reflects the desire of every godly parent for our children and grandchildren, as well as the kids in our churches, schools, and neighborhoods. I feel as if I prayed this prayer nearly every time I held my son or one of my three daughters in my arms. But notice David's motivation for praying that prayer, the relational foundation that prompted his prayer: "For your love for me is very great" (Psalm 86:13 NLT).

Not long ago, Dartmouth Medical School commissioned a scientific study of young people. However, rather than generating new research, this project analyzed the results of more than 260 current scientific studies of young people. The results were so revealing, they prompted the project to be renamed. "A Scientific Study of Young People" became "Hardwired to Connect."[5] Why the change? Because, they said, all the research—not 90 percent, not 95, not even 99 percent, but all of it—showed that from the moment a baby is born, that child's brain is physically, biologically, chemically hardwired to connect with others in relationships. That's the case not only spiritually and emotionally but also physiologically.

Do you want to pass your values on to young people? Do you want your children to come to know your Savior? Do you want the next generation to grasp and live biblical truth? If so scientific research says you must do two things: (1) Build loving, intimate connections, relationships with children, or they will almost certainly reject the truth you care about, and (2) model that very value or truth in the presence of those young people.

Relationships engender belief. Jesus spent three years with His first disciples, eating with them, laughing and crying with them, traveling with them, sleeping next to them, teaching them, correcting them, and building a relational foundation for the day when He would say to them, "I have given you an example to follow. Do as I have done to you" (John 13:15 NLT).

Likewise, Paul established a relationship with people in Philippi, including a merchant named Lydia and her family and a Roman jailer and his family. He and the others in his party lodged with them, ate with them, performed miracles in their midst, and endured persecution with them, providing the relational basis for Paul's words years later: "Pattern your lives after mine, and learn from those who follow our example" (Philippians 3:17 NLT).

Jesus and Paul both clearly foreshadowed the model recommended by twenty-first-century scientific research: Relationship engenders belief.

Where Relationship Is Lacking

After the tragic shootings at Columbine High School, which claimed 13 lives, Columbia University commissioned a study. The objective was to find out if (and how) family structure affected a child's involvement in drugs and alcohol, and whether that had any impact on that child's potential for violent behavior. Here is a portion of the study's findings:

- In a single-parent home where the mother is the head of the home, a child is 30 percent more likely to become involved in drugs, alcohol, and violence.

- In a two-parent biological home, but where there is a fairly poor relationship with the father, a child is 68 percent likely to become involved in drugs, alcohol, and violence.

- In a two-parent biological home where the child has a good to excellent relationship with the father, a child is less than 6 percent likely to become involved in drugs, alcohol, or violence.[6]

According to that study, not only the structure of a family but also the strength of the relationships within the family produces the likelihood of certain behaviors. Relationships engender our beliefs. Beliefs then contribute to the formation of our values, which in turn drive our behavior:

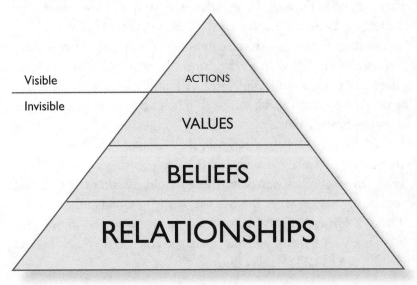

Another study performed after the Columbine tragedy was commissioned by the FBI. The purpose of this study was to see if a profile could be reliably established that would help teachers, administrators, police, and others to detect potential shooters. It's called the Classroom Avenger profile.[7] Researchers carefully studied the lives of 17 previous school shooters and found three main distinctives: Every shooter was white, middle-class, and from a home in which the father was either absent, distant, or not involved in the parenting process. Relationships engender the beliefs that form our values and drive our behavior.

Johns Hopkins commissioned two doctors to identify any contributing factors for five diseases or conditions (mental illness, hypertension, malignant tumors, heart disease, and suicide) in peoples lives. In other words, would it be possible to say, if A or B were true in a child's life, that child would be more likely to experience any of these things later in life? After 30 years of research involving 1377 graduates, they found only one common factor among these conditions. It wasn't diet (thank God). It wasn't exercise (hallelujah!). Remarkably, the sole common link was the lack of closeness to one's parents, especially the father.[8]

Don't feel badly if you find that incredible. I did too at first. So I called Johns Hopkins, and when they couldn't answer my questions, they connected me with the authors of the study, who took only a few minutes to persuade me that the lack of closeness to one's parents—especially to the father—is the common contributing factor to those five conditions. Why? In a word: stress. In other words, they found that a child raised in a loving, intimate family relationship, especially with the father, can handle stress so much better as they grow older. Relationships are the key.

Not long ago, Michael Jackson, the "King of Pop," shared something that happened in his first rehearsal as lead singer of the Jackson Five, when Michael was only five years old. During the rehearsal, something went wrong, and Michael turned around and called out, "Daddy!" His father abruptly stopped the rehearsal and sternly said, "I am not your father! I am your manager! And don't you ever forget that." Michael said he never did.

More recently, while speaking at Oxford University in England to about 800 students and professors, Jackson was speaking about Help the Children, the foundation he started. Just minutes into his talk, he broke down in tears. When he regained his composure a few minutes later, he explained, "I just wanted a dad. A father who showed me love, and my father never did that. He never once said, 'Michael, I love you.'" Relationships engender the beliefs that form our values and in turn drive our behavior.

Hugh Hefner, founder of the *Playboy* publishing empire, has given many interviews about his hedonistic lifestyle. Yet I have never heard him reference his father, and only once did I hear him talk about his mother. In a cable news interview, he said, "I knew my mother loved me, but she never expressed it. So I had to learn about love from the movies." He seemed to be saying that his belief system and value system lacked a relational foundation.

I've tried to do exactly the opposite in raising my children. Whenever the need for a healthy dose of truth arose with my kids—for example, when some lesson or discipline was called for—I tried to firmly place it in the context of my relationship with them. My first words were always, "Do you know that I love you?" Because, of course, the answer to that question was an all-important antecedent to the effective transmission of truth. Before ever dealing with issues or attitudes in my children, I first cemented the relationship and only then went on to deal with the problems—still in the context of the relationship. Relationships engender belief.

A Biblical Apologetic

Remember the pastor whose church boasted about preaching "the truth—and the truth only"? When I explained to him that it was not the proclamation of truth that turned the world upside down, he bristled.

"Sure it was," he said.

I smiled and shook my head. "No, it wasn't," I said.

You see, what happened in the first century—and the task we face today, as well—involved far more than a strictly modernist approach, which appeals to the intellect. It also involved more than an extreme postmodern approach, which treats the truth as an irrelevance. Our first-century forebears would be unsatisfied with both modernism, which exalts truth but minimizes relationships, and postmodernism, which minimizes truth and exalts relationships. Truth without relationships is modernism. Relationships without truth is postmodernism. The world we live in—the great host of people all around us—is desperate for truth that is firmly grasped, grounded, and communicated in the context of relationships.

"Preaching the truth is not what turned the world upside down," I explained to that pastor. "It was a thoroughly biblical apologetic, neither modern nor postmodern." It's what Paul referred to when he depicted the process that brought the Thessalonians to a vibrant faith in Christ: "Having so fond an affection for you, we were well-pleased to impart to you not only the gospel of God but also our own lives, because you had become very dear to us" (1 Thessalonians 2:8).

That's what turned the world upside down in the first days of church history! It was an apologetic exemplified in those first Christians' willingness to impart not only the truth but also their very lives. Their apologetic was not "truth only." It was not modernism. Not postmodernism. It was truth in the context of relationships. The way they lived their lives was further proof of the truth of the message (1 Thessalonians 1:5 NLT).

Writing to the church at Rome, Paul said, "For I will not presume to speak of anything except what Christ has accomplished through me, resulting in the obedience of the Gentiles by word and deed" (Romans 15:18 NLT).

Paul's apologetic was richer than modernism and fuller than postmodernism. It was clearly two-pronged: People were drawn to the gospel by the truth in the context of relationship.

In his book *They Like Jesus but Not the Church,* Dan Kimball dedicates a chapter to discussing "What They Wish the Church Were Like"—that is, what non-Christians and nonchurchgoers say would make the Christian faith attractive and perhaps even irresistible. These are two of the most common answers he discusses: "I wish the church were a loving place," and "I wish the church would respect my intelligence." Both are crucial.

That's My Story (And I'm Sticking with It)

Most people assume I came to Christ through the intellectual route. Certainly, there can't be more than a few people who have documented more evidences for the faith than I have. And yet, all the evidence I have documented—on the reliability of the Bible, the deity of Jesus Christ, and the evidence for the resurrection—never brought me to faith in Christ.

That's right. The evidences did not bring me to Christ. The evidences got my attention, but it was God's love that drew me. It was the love I saw between a group of genuine believers who loved not only Jesus Christ but also each other—and even me!

The evidence got my attention, but love drew me. When I think back to that night when I realized it, I still get chills. It was Saturday night in a university dorm. I was a total skeptic and an absolute heathen. Only God and the Holy Spirit could have shown me that if I were the only person alive, Jesus still would have died for me.

I've said often that I grew up with a father who was the town drunk. I've told how I had to watch him beat my mother. I've shared that I hated him and took my revenge on him when I got old enough and strong enough. But I never shared the following until recently.

Between the ages of six and thirteen, I was severely sexually abused by a man named Wayne Bailey. When I was six years old, he was hired on the farm to be a cook and a housekeeper. Whenever my mother would leave or my folks would go downtown or go away for a few days, my mother would always march me to Wayne Bailey and say, "Now, you obey Wayne. You do everything that he tells you to do or you'll get a thrashing when I get home." So I was at Wayne Bailey's mercy.

When I was nine years old, and again at the age of twelve, I told my mother what had been going on. She didn't believe me. I can't describe the pain and abandonment I felt, on top of the abuse, when my own mother refused to believe me.

Finally, however, at thirteen years of age, I was strong enough. My parents had left for the weekend, and I went into the house and backed this man against the wall.

"If you ever touch me again," I said, "I will kill you."

And I would have. Two weeks later, he left. I remember my mom and dad talking that night around the dinner table. They asked each other, "I wonder what happened? Why did he leave? Why didn't he give notice?"

I sat there thinking, *Why didn't you believe me?*

Wayne was gone, but of course by that time, the damage had been done. I had nothing going for me and everything going against me. A worse-than-absent father. Abandoned by my mother. And horribly abused on top of it all. I should have become the victim of victims.

But when I arrived at Kellogg College in Battle Creek, Michigan, I met a group of Christians who exposed me for the first time to the love of God. Oh, how they loved each other. And I wanted what they had so badly that I would have paid anything for it. I would have pawned my soul to have what they had. That love—and the desire for that kind of relationship—paved the road of faith for me, and thus began my journey of faith.

Some time later, I met the pastor of a tiny church, Factorville Bible Church. I went to him and shared what had happened to me. And he believed me! I can't tell you what that meant. It was like being born again…again. He believed me!

For six months after that, he walked me through Scripture after Scripture, verse after verse, on forgiveness. When he finished and finally said, "Josh, you need to forgive him," I answered, "No way." I wanted him to burn in hell, and I wanted to escort him there.

Obviously, if I had not encountered God's love in that student group at Kellogg College and experienced it again through that pastor's friendship and mentoring, I would have been content to hate Wayne

Bailey for the rest of my life. But the truth had taken root in me as a result of those relationships. I'm convinced that all the evidence in the world, all the most powerful arguments and most convincing proofs, would never have gotten through to me if the transforming power of God's love had not reached my heart through that student group and others, including the pastor of tiny Factorville Bible Church. In fact, my mind continued to rebel long after my heart knew what I must do.

But, steeled by that pastor's loving support, one day I found out where Wayne Bailey lived. I drove to his house. I knocked on his door. I introduced myself. And, though I must admit I didn't want to tell him because I didn't want it to be true, I forgave Wayne Bailey and told him that Jesus died for him as much as He did for me.

The Ring of Truth

What was true of the Philippians and Thessalonians—and me—is true of our children, grandchildren, students, neighbors, coworkers, friends, and family members. They are desperate for truth that is firmly grasped, grounded, and communicated in the context of relationships. As Paul said, "If I could speak all the languages of earth and of angels, but didn't love others, I would only be a noisy gong or a clanging cymbal" (1 Corinthians 13:1 NLT).

According to the research, that's what our proclamation of truth has sounded like to the world around us: a meaningless noise. Our message is falling on deaf ears to the world around us because we are too often delivering the truth—and the truth only, unfortunately.

We need a new approach, a fresh apologetic, though it's actually as old as the church. It's how Jesus trained His first followers. It's the way Paul won a Philippian merchant and jailer to the faith. It's the route by which Jason and others from Thessalonica were drawn to Christ. And it's the path I took as well.

It's not modernism. It's not postmodernism. It's not relationships and it's not truth, not one or the other. It is a thoroughly biblical apologetic: truth in the context of relationships, an apologetic that acknowledges and capitalizes on the fact that truth bears the sweetest fruit when it is planted in the soil of a loving relationship.

Josh McDowell is the author or coauthor of more than 108 books, including *More Than a Carpenter* and *The New Evidence That Demands a Verdict.*

CHRISTIANITY AND CULTURE: DEFENDING OUR FATHERS AND MOTHERS

by John Mark Reynolds

Making It Likely: The Importance of Cultural Apologetics

This week I stood in two churches. One was tiny but full of worshippers. It was battered, but the members were slowly restoring it. There was a humble confidence of the faces of the members. The choir consisted of people drawn from the area.

The other church was gigantic but nearly empty. Most of the people in the chairs were tourists, and the smell of cultural irrelevance was in the air. The choir was perfect but professional, and the service was perfect but passionless.

The first church stood just apart from the Alexander Palace. It was the church home of the martyred royal family of Russia. The second church was Westminster Abbey, where the ruling English royals go for many of their marriages and burials.

A church nearly extinct under a ferocious wave of persecution that sent millions to death shows faint but hopeful signs of revival. A church that survived two world wars, endured great economic turmoil, and sent great Christian leaders to much of the rest of Christendom is fading. Some predict that many Christian groups will vanish, or very nearly so, in the next 50 years.

In 1918 the situation would have seemed the reverse. The church of

Russia faced extinction, and the church in Britain, revival. The young were of the new Soviet Union, and they helped their atheistic regime blow up priceless churches and replace them with swimming holes. Many of the young of the British Isles joined a wave of missionaries reaching out in a stream of evangelism that continues today.

Cultures can change—quickly. Why should we care? We care about cultures because we care about people. Bad cultures hurt people, and good cultures help them. Apologists for our new generation must study culture to help find ways to make things better.

Bad cultures reward vice while good cultures punish it. Good cultures can make the ideas of Christianity more palatable to many people by preparing their imaginations for it. A person reared on fairy tales, Narnia stories, and Sunday school is more likely to be found in church as an adult than a child whose first touch of wonder is warped by thousands of advertisements, video games like Grand Theft Auto, and pornography on the Internet.

Cultures Matter: No Christ Without Christendom

Why should Christians care about our culture? Isn't it our business to live our lives quietly and witness to our faith as we can? Isn't the whole idea of Christendom passé or dangerous? Christians must care about the culture for four reasons.

First, creating a culture that embodies the values of Christ's kingdom on this earth is unavoidable for a Christian. We are the King's men and women, and we act in His name. Even in non-Christian (or post-Christian) lands, by merely living well, Christians form a counterculture to whatever non-Christians are doing. Living such countercultural lives is one way we can lift up the name of Jesus. This counterculture will complement and in some cases compete with the secular society.

Second, to create is part of human nature. God made us in His image. Father God is a creator, and His children share that nature. We create because He first created. The act of creation is frequently a collaborative process. Communities form around the act of making something beautiful, and over time many such communities form a culture. Even the solitary Christian artist creates for God and is honored for this act of worship by believers either in his lifetime or later.

Third, caring about culture honors our spiritual fathers and mothers. We discredit our spiritual parents by ignoring the cultural gifts they gave us while mindlessly benefiting from them. Some Christians wish to expose the spiritual nakedness and errors of our forebears in order to curry favor with the dominant powers of our age. These Christians seem to have forgotten that those institutions stand on the faith community's cultural achievements. There is no Christian who does not live in Christ's kingdom, Christendom.

Finally, great cultures become long-term witnesses to the truth of the gospel. When atheists ruled Russia, they did so in a Kremlin dominated by churches too beautiful for even Stalin to destroy. If the living Christian witness vanishes altogether in Britain, the most beautiful buildings in Oxford and Cambridge will continue to proclaim the glory of God in stained glass and stone. Sadly, too many American Christians are leaving nothing behind, spending all their spiritual resources now while leaving nothing culturally for future generations.

Learning the Whole Story: The Truth About Christendom

If you are embarrassed by your heritage or worry that it is corrupt, this can destroy your confidence to act based on that history. One way bigots and tyrants try to oppress a people is to destroy their knowledge and pride in their heritage. This is the tactic of the so-called New Atheists.

Obviously this patrimony is complicated and contains both shameful and honorable deeds. We are the people of the great cathedrals but also of the tortures of the Inquisition. The religious fervor that produced the American genius Jonathan Edwards also produced the Salem witch trials. Sadly, most of the students in universities I meet have heard of the bad things we have done but not the good. Secular schools have shamed us into silence. After all, if Christendom were mostly bad for the world, then decency requires that we withdraw from the public square.

Humility about our history is in order, but extremists in the secular community insist we feel nothing but shame. This is unnecessary because the good of Christendom far outweighs the bad, just as good and honorable ministers outnumber the hypocrites.

Christianity has suffered great persecution since its inception, but it has also been weakened by fools and knaves who used the faith as a means to do great harm. Christians have done some bad things (which should not be too surprising because we're all still sinners), but the legacy of Christianity is overwhelmingly positive. Christians often do not know this, or they believe the opposite!

If they know anything about the medieval period, for example, they may know about the Inquisition, but they may not know about the great contributions to international law the church courts made in that time. They may not know the slow and steady progress Christians made in creating systems that would protect the rights of the accused. They may know about the tortures but not about the Christian arguments that ended torture.

Christians must educate themselves in their own heritage. Christian thinkers had a seminal role in the creation of science. Christians created the modern hospital systems and the basis for the modern university. Christian states slowly learned to treat believers in other states as brothers and sisters. We abolished slavery and elevated the rights of the poor and the oppressed. We are the religion of Augustine, Aquinas, Dante, Rembrandt, and Bach. Apologists for our new generation must be aware of the remarkable contribution Christianity has made to science, ethics, government, economics, and more.[1]

Building Christendom:
A Necessary Commitment to Reason and Beauty

Worse than the bad ideas that come to Christians from the outside are the falsehoods we tell ourselves. In my experience, the most important mistakes American Christians make about culture relate to reason and beauty. We wrongly believe that we should be hostile to reason and ignore beauty as unimportant. These errors have had many sad consequences, not the least of which is a loss of hope in the promise of cultural renewal. As a result of our retreat from reason and beauty, Christians have lost certain cultural arguments for so long that they assume they must always lose them!

A Commitment to Reason

Christians today commonly consider faith to be a belief in something despite the evidence or even *because* all the evidence is against it. This is not, however, the faith of Paul, who gave careful evidence for his belief in the physical resurrection of Jesus Christ from the dead. Biblical faith is (among other things) a reasonable belief in the truth of an uncertain proposition. Faith makes decisions based on the provisional acceptance of ideas that could be wrong but that the believer has good reasons to believe are true.

Understood in this traditionally Christian manner, faith is a friend to reason. From Augustine to Aquinas to C.S. Lewis, the story of Christian thought is overwhelmingly the story of men and women testing their provisional faith commitments to make sure they are reasonable. Christians do not have equal amounts of faith in all their religious commitments. We have much better evidence for believing in the resurrection of Jesus Christ from the dead, for example, than we have for the singular miracle at Cana of Galilee. The first is more central to Christianity than the second, so this is not surprising or threatening. The evidence for both events is complimentary and mutually reinforcing, but we have more compelling reasons to give for Jesus being alive today than we have (or even need!) for His turning water to wine.

Being reasonable is an attempt to make one's beliefs correspond to the truth. One tool of reasonable thinking is logic. Logic is simply an attempt to develop rules of reason to avoid bad thinking. As a series of rules about right reasoning, logic can help a person find truth, but it does not deal directly with truth itself.

An argument usually consists of two parts: premises (reasons) and a conclusion. A good argument will contain true premises (good reasons) and will also be valid. Logic helps us discover patterns of *valid* arguments. In a valid argument, if the premises are true, the conclusion cannot be false. A valid argument is often very valuable because it may take propositions we already know to be true, combine them, and produce a conclusion that we might not have accepted before the argument was made.

There should be no exceptions made to the rules of right reason. Logical rules are not secular (in the sense they have nothing to do with God); rather, they show us how God thinks (as best we can tell). There is good reason that the apostle John calls the second person of the Trinity the divine Word, which can also be understood as the divine Logic.

No good Christian should ever intentionally make an invalid argument. It is a kind of impiety for a man made in the image of God to sully that image by refusing to be a person of logic. Sadly, though making valid arguments is relatively easy, finding the truth can be difficult. Christians believe truth can be found through reason, traditional experience, and revelation. There is no shortcut to carefully examining what we believe or any easy way out of the moral obligation to do so. Logic is part of our heritage. Every human is made in God's image, so Christians are not the only ones to love logic or to participate in its discovery. As followers of the Logos, however, we have particular reasons for taking it seriously. From Anselm to Alvin Plantinga, Christians have found our religion a particular motivation to try to make persuasive arguments. This is not only for apologetic or utilitarian reasons but also from the very nature of the divine image stamped in mankind.

We should love reason because we love God. A good sign for a properly developing Christian culture is its commitment to reason. Another such test is the commitment of the Christian to beauty and a rejection of ugliness.

A Commitment to Beauty

Ugliness is a bad sign for the truth of an idea. When the Word became flesh, we beheld His glory. Thank God He did not appear as so many utilitarian churches appear today! On their good days, the followers of Jesus Christ burst with beauty and romance. We created Rococo and Gothic art and architecture. Whenever Christianity begins to fade, men begin to become severe, harsh, and practical. They begin to limit the number of holidays and sniff at anything impractical.

We see this not only in defective Christian culture but also in Russian secularism. Every year of communism saw ever more severe and practical concrete flats being foisted on colorful Saint Petersburg. The czars, however imperfect, built the candy-striped onion domes, but the atheist planners built colorless and drab monstrosities. One need only compare the Spanish mission churches in California to later civic buildings to see the general truth that beauty follows truth and flees error.

In Christian circles, the reality of goodness is not often called into question. Morality is grounded in divinity, revealed in the Word of God, and lived out in the community of faith. Christians believe goodness would exist even if there were no humans. Morality is not the creation of men, but of God.

In both Christian and popular secular circles, almost everybody agrees that beauty is a matter of opinion. Begin a sentence, "Beauty is…" and most will end it with "in the eye of the beholder." As recently as C.S. Lewis however, Christians were still relatively united on the existence of objective beauty (either as an idea on its own or in God's mind). This is a remarkable change. The belief that beauty is subjective has become almost universal. It is understandable why those who reject absolute goodness, truth, and beauty as an explicit part of traditional Western theism would deny the objective reality of beauty, but why did Christians accept this major change?

As Lewis suggests in *Abolition of Man,* the shift away from objective beauty was accomplished in the lower grades of schools. Without much argument, it appeared at an early stage of the curriculum with teachers who were usually unaware of the implications of what they were teaching. I experienced this myself.

When in fifth grade, I was given a "fact-opinion" worksheet in English class, as were many other students in primary schools in the United States. On this sheet, I was taught to distinguish between fact and opinion. Facts included statements such as "Lyndon Johnson was president of the United States." Opinions included statements such as "A rose is beautiful." As C.S. Lewis points out in *Abolition of Man,* the most important essay of the twentieth century, lessons were being taught to me that had nothing to do with English. Essentially without any argument, beauty was declared subjective and just a matter of personal opinion.

A consumer culture also encourages a passive acceptance of subjective beauty. After all, companies want to move product. If beauty is in the eye of the beholder, then mass media might be able to determine what beauty is. They do not have economic interest in maintaining classical standards over time, but they have a high motivation to cater to personal tastes. Companies exist to give the customer what he or she desires, not to educate them in what they should desire!

Is it any wonder that music, theater, and art are vanishing from education? The sciences and mathematics use beauty (or elegance) as one way of weighing the merit of a solution, but beauty is the special province of the arts. A subjective view of beauty has been most costly there. Science is protected by pragmatic concerns, but the arts seem much less practical to many.

The arts are vanishing from education before college for the non-specialist and are under severe pressure as useless and expensive in the university. This is to be expected if beauty is merely a matter of preference and opinion. Why should the government pay to let some beholders teach their preferences to other beholders?

This is in marked contrast to the Christian tradition regarding the arts. The traditional Christian school views the arts as vital because they help educate about the nature of beauty. We must reclaim the importance of beauty in a Christian education. Christians must pay attention to what artists and musicians are saying. We must value beauty for its own sake as part of a fully human life lived in praise of God. Apologetics training for our new generation must include an appreciation of new arts such as film in addition to a general education in the fine arts. Only in this way can we begin to live more fully Christian lives. Most of all, we must regain the hope that such positive changes are still possible. Too many Christians assume that our present cultural defeats can only continue.

Living in Hope

The comparison of our own sense of despair with that of Christians in the former Soviet Union is a telling one. Even when the Soviet Union was on its last legs, many people did not see the change coming and felt hopeless before the Bolshevik menace. They assumed that the bad news would just keep coming for Christians. They lost hope. That is a bad idea because the kingdom of Christ endures against every adversary. Just as the church outlasted the Soviet Union, so it will endure the hedonism, materialism, and the antichrist spirit of our own time.

Present cultural trends will not continue forever. Humans are no more capable of consistency in their wicked deeds than in their good! Things change. What was trendy yesterday becomes the establishment of tomorrow and will soon be supplanted. Christians need never lose hope, because though we may appear to be losing, new ideologies will not last forever.

All is not lost, for even when all seems lost, God still governs the world. As usual, Christians today live in dark times. What should Christians do in the light of the particular cultural problems we face? We must abandon our fears and become ambassadors of Christendom to the culture. We must ask the right questions of ourselves and our communities. Christians should embrace the importance of beauty and be motivated (always!) by love. Finally, we should create and not just consume culture. The first step is getting the right attitude.

The worst thing most Christians can do is to be afraid of the times. There is, as the Bible reminds us, no fear in love, and we are to be motivated always by love. Some of us may be called to set up retreats where quiet and rest is the rule. Most of us, however, will be called to live where the people are and serve them in the midst of their cities. Jesus is Lord, so fear has no place in this job. Even if our section of a culture seems in total rebellion to God and His Christ, it cannot be. Any good it does is done because of God's image in people. Any evil it can do is only a twisting of the good world God created.

The weakness of evil is that it exists only as a twisting of good or as a shadow. If we turn up the light, the shadows will flee. Most of Western culture is a guttering flame or bent reed. Too many Christians seem eager to finish off the job and blow out the light or break the reed. God may indeed judge a culture, but our job is rarely (if ever!) to be His instruments of judgment.

The role of God's people is to offer hope for reconciliation that comes from God to mankind. This is true in the arts, science, politics, and every other area of human endeavor. If we look carefully, we will see some good news in every object of art or culture. The better the art of the thing, the more Christian it will be.

How can we practically become reconcilers of the culture to Christ? How can we imitate Christ in making (through the power of the Holy Spirit) the crooked straight? These are a few of the right questions Christians can begin to ask in our church communities.

When Jesus met two of His disciples after He rose from the dead, He did not immediately meet their felt need. Instead, the great Teacher asked them questions. Why did the Lord Jesus do this? He wanted to meet people's real need and not merely the needs they understood they had.

These right questions require the right context. Christians must embrace the fundamental value of beauty. It is time for our works to match our words. We read a sublimely beautiful Book, and this should motivate us to make everything in our lives match the nature of the Word of God.

Christ and His Kingdom

In my book *When Athens Met Jerusalem,* I show how Christianity solved the problems of the Greek and Roman culture it encountered. Philosophy had reached a dead end regarding the relationship of religion, beauty, and reason. Christianity provided the answer. The Incarnation, where God became man, was the solution to certain problems that had escaped even Plato. Just as important was the fact that Christianity was also attractive to the lower classes of the Roman Empire. It was a way of thinking that could almost uniquely bring together sage and slave. This triumph should encourage us today.

Our time is no darker than the first century because human wickedness is no different than it ever was. The problems and virtues of our own age will look almost attractive to the generation to come, just as we admire our spiritual fathers' and mothers' heroism and no longer fear the threats they faced.

Any great civilization will be built on ideas it found from direct contact with Christ's church or from the common grace and image of God given to all mankind. Christendom, Christ's kingdom, like her master, was, is, and is to come. Christians need not be afraid, and non-Christians should consider joining the winning cause.

Christendom can be unattractive when it wins, but the alternative is always worse. In every place the church labors hard to build an earthly image of Jerusalem. We are imperfect, so each state holds the seeds of its own destruction. Waiting at the edges of each culture is a bloodthirsty revolutionary like a latter-day Robespierre or Lenin, waiting to parasitically profit on the good the church has done while destroying the culture's fecundity.

This is as true in a town as in a nation, in a church as in a denomination. Nothing the faithful can build this side of paradise will last forever. Every Camelot has a Mordred. Every generation must ask whether it will renew its covenant with the Almighty and so revive its hopes for further greatness, or plunge into decadence, destroying so much for some short-term gain.

Will the next generation of Christians bless us, or will they wonder how we let so much slip away?

John Mark Reynolds is the founder and director of the Torrey Honors Institute at Biola University and a founder of Wheatstone Academy, a classical summer educational program.

AN INTERVIEW WITH J.P. MORELAND

Sean McDowell: Why is it important to train people to defend their beliefs today?

J.P. Moreland: Everyone wants to have beliefs that make sense. You don't buy a house if you have absolutely no idea whatsoever if it has holes in the roof. In any decision you make in life, you at least try to look into it enough to decide whether it's a sensible decision. This shouldn't be any different with God. If we're trying to decide if we are going to give our lives for this, we should care as to whether anything can be said for it. Apologetics is a ministry of helping people overcome barriers to belief or to growing in their belief.

Sean: Does apologetics help with evangelism?

J.P.: Here is the key question: How do you develop people who have the kind of confidence and courage to abandon their whole lives to Christ, who really want to change the world, backing it up with their actions? You don't do it by having a faith that's true for me, and maybe not true for you. I challenge anyone who opts for that approach to discipleship to look and see if the people who are being nurtured in that kind of environment are radically committed to change the world for Christ and getting after it out there among the unbelieving world. On the other hand, if you find people who have received a little bit of training in defending their faith—their evangelism, their courage—they're becoming radical and countercultural.

Sean: Can we argue people into the kingdom?

J.P.: Can you force people to become Christians with an argument? No. Nothing you can do except put a gun to their heads, perhaps, would force people to become Christians. But apologetics isn't about forcing people to do anything. Apologetics simply helps people find answers if they've got obstacles or difficulties in their hearts and lives.

Sean: Why do apologetics sometimes get criticized?

J.P.: First, people often misunderstand what it means to do apologetics. Many people associate apologetics with a cold, objective, didactic presentation of the facts that is meant to control what people believe. If that's what apologetics were about, you could count me out as well! This overlooks the type of reasoning of *The Chronicles of Narnia* by C.S. Lewis, which is presented in story form in a very warm, passionate way. You can even engage in apologetics through presenting your own testimony while including some of the reasons you found persuasive.

Second, in a culture where people are not well-educated any longer, where they know deep in their hearts that they cannot think very well, or they know they really don't know why they believe what they believe, it's too painful to admit they are inadequate and need to grow. Some people also don't want to do their homework to make progress.

Sean: What happens to Christians who don't know why they believe what they believe?

J.P.: They tend to retreat to a form of personal subjectivism or to a safe ground where they can't be interrogated any further. Or they will use the Bible in a way it was never intended—as a trump card. They'll say, "That's what the Bible says, and that's the end of the story." If you look in the book of Acts and observe how the apostles did evangelism, they didn't say, "Listen. Believe me. I'm an apostle. The words I'm saying are inspired by God. That settles it." Rather, they reasoned with people.

> **J.P. Moreland** is distinguished professor of philosophy at Talbot School of Theology and the author of many books, including *Kingdom Triangle.*

A HUMAN APOLOGETIC:
TILLING THE SOUL

by Dale Fincher

How can apologetics assist us in soul formation? The general consensus among evangelicals is that apologetics is for the academic types, those who fearlessly dissolve attacks against the Christian faith, debate headliner atheists, and distribute literature on *The Da Vinci Code*. But we need to think beyond these boundaries.

Apologetics is simply an answer or defense. But an answer for what? An answer for the claims of Christian faith, for sure. But what about an answer for the hunger in our souls? An answer for what it means to be human? An answer for how we can live contrary to the systems of this world? All these questions are included as we reimagine apologetics for the next generation.

Apologetics is an invitation, even to those of us who never got good grades in school. Jesus said that one of the key points to human existence is not simply to have truth but to be free (John 8:32). We want truth so that our souls will be transformed.

And soul formation—what is that? It is growing in friendship with God by developing the same kind of inner life that Jesus had, His kinds of thoughts and emotions, His courage to follow the will of His Father. Soul formation is freedom—liberty to be ourselves.

So why does apologetics seem like it's only for the intellectually gifted? In the twentieth century, two different kinds of apologetics took the stage. In the twenty-first century, a new apologetic will draw the two together and invite others into the conversation.

Those two traditions are entwined in my own journey. One focused on the life of the analytic mind of the intellectual types, and the other focused on the way truth fosters the human imagination and makes us more human. The former is specialized; the latter is more generalized. The former is expressed in academic essays; the latter creates a culture that draws on imagination and human experience.[1] The former gives truth; the latter gives meaning to truth.

I attended Talbot School of Theology and earned an M.A. in the challenging Philosophy of Religion and Ethics department. It leaned heavily on the analytic approach, and I learned how to clearly formulate an argument.

Yet something was missing for me. Though I learned the nitty-gritty of epistemology and the philosophy of science, I thirsted for something more.

One semester, I supplemented my studies by rereading C.S. Lewis. Lewis reminded me that truth creates a satisfaction in the world, an amazement in beauty and goodness, a gladness to be alive! He helped me see the analytic and the imaginative at the same time, a way forward that was both relevant to my world but also more human, body and soul. I'd like to call his tradition "humanitarian apologetics."

Our apologetic must be human and not merely abstract concepts if our souls are to be changed. And humanitarian apologetics can only be partly taught. It requires a deeper involvement of the soul saturated in emotional health. It requires an approach that is personal, both with the person sharing and the Person being shared. It requires that we refresh why we are here on this planet and then make that an integral part of our vocabulary. It integrates philosophy, theology, and science as well as the breadth of the humanities and social justice.

We need to link the soul with life. I am surprised that many of the next generation do not make the connection between truth and life. They want the good life, like an amateur climber eyeing a mountaintop. Yet truth, like climbing gear in their backpack, goes unused because they don't see its usefulness. They don't know how the gear connects with the mountain. Jesus quite often compared the good news to a change in quality of life: living water, good shepherds, rich fields, abundant crops, and priceless pearls. Our apologetic should form the soul with Jesus' abundant life. Apologetics formed my soul in many ways. I want to share four to spur you on.

Apologetics Cultivates the Garden of Our Beliefs

My wife and I launched a nonprofit organization in the spring of 2005 called Soulation. This is our tag line: "Sturdy answers. Better souls." We both felt that plenty of apologists out there developed intellectually but didn't value the emotional and volitional life of human beings. We wanted to merge all three.

My soul is what I am. I am a soul that has a body. My soul holds my mind, my emotions, and my will. And I inform and am informed by my body. Our souls take their proper shape as we are forged into the design God intended for us from the beginning as whole, healthy humans.

Our mind is like a garden sprouting up with beliefs. What sprouts in that garden leads to the nourishment or malnutrition of our souls. A false belief—such as a conviction that God is fickle—withers my soul. A true belief—such as a conviction that I am valuable because I'm made in God's image—makes my soul blossom. In other words, what we believe largely effects who we become.

The enemy knows this. He ensnares human souls by planting weeds of false beliefs. That is why Paul writes, "Be transformed by the renewing of your mind" (Romans 12:2). But what is a renewed mind? It's a refreshed mind, replanted with God's way of seeing things. To paraphrase Paul, "We weed out arguments and every pretension that plants itself against the knowledge of God, and with every thought we push the roots of our beliefs deeper in life-giving obedience to Christ" (2 Corinthians 10:5).

The enemy wages spiritual battle to skew our knowledge of God. He is not primarily trying to get us to raise our fists against God.

Rather he's trying to change our view of God, to get us to bow the knee to a god that is not there. If he can poison our idea of God by tempting us to project our view of our parents or of churchgoers or of our self-designed spirituality on God, then he succeeds. A.W. Tozer said, "What comes into our minds when we think about God is the most important thing about us." It reveals the flourishing (or stagnation) in our souls.

Apologetics examines our false beliefs, refreshing and fertilizing an accurate picture of what God is like and what He is up to with the whole world. My Talbot colleague and friend Gary Osmundsen has reminded me, "Truth is one way God shows His love toward us." Truth is part of God's companionship, part of His love coming near and drawing us out. Accepting truth is accepting a person. My wife might tell me that she'd like to have fresh flowers on Valentine's Day, regardless of how much I tell her that they won't last. By accepting this truth about her, I'm accepting her for who she is. As Kent Hill points out, the acceptance of truth, and not merely its discovery, changes the soul.

How Knowledge Works

Students have asked me, "How do I have more faith and become less selfish and more loving?" That question requires apologetics to get at the root of change. Knowledge of God and ourselves will grow deep roots. Only then will branches of faith and love sprout and grow.

After speaking to a large group of parents about teens and faith, I received this question from a sincere mother: "How can I teach my children about truth when I'm trying to teach them about faith?"

The Bible assumes our faith grows as our knowledge grows. This is contrary to a modern, secular notion of faith—a view that many (if not most) people in the church today have. Faith is sometimes defined as believing against the facts. Biblical faith is trust, the kind of trust you experience in a friendship. Faith trusts a person shown to be worthy of trust. But how can I have faith in someone I do not know? If I don't have knowledge of who God is, my soul cannot grow in trusting Him.

If the secular view of faith is correct, I should ask God never to grant my prayers so I can grow to believe in Him against the facts. In the biblical model, faith grows when God answers our prayers because we know God better. We see His character and trust Him more.

Like faith, love also requires knowledge to grow. According to popular notions about love, the more I work on my feelings of love, the greater my love will be. This view is causing many in the next generation to flounder in their commitments.

Love needs knowledge. I've seen this in my marriage. The more I know Jonalyn, the more I know how to love her. God generously gives us those feelings of attraction and infatuation early in our romance to lead us into the wild and scary adventure of love. As the feelings ebb and flow, we press more deeply into who it is we are loving. To love is to will the good of another. But I must know Jonalyn to know what her good is. Jonalyn and I committed early on to become scholars of one another, and that has paid off. I love her more than the day I met her because I know her more.

The same is true in your relationship with God. If you want to love Him more, you must know Him more and know what it means to will His good. The Lord's Prayer says, "Thy kingdom come, Thy will be done." Why? Because this is for the good of God, to bring His kingdom on earth as it is in heaven.

Apologetics Invites Us to Ask Our Troubling Questions

My questions ran hot and deep in my teen years. I wasn't merely curious when I asked, "What is the best way to live?" or "Does God exist?" Answers for spiritual trivia were intriguing, but answers that quenched the thirst in my soul were my salvation.

Those who have tossed and turned on their pillows, agitated and feeling horribly lost in a strange world, know the anguish that comes from unhinged questions. "Fear" is a good word for it: fear of being alone with no way out.

Today I realize why people overlooked my struggle, misunderstood it, and interpreted it as rebellion. Those soul questions were hidden.

We know about relief efforts that rush to the rescue of those who are physically suffering. We rightly view firemen as heroes! But who are the heroes to rescue those who are intellectually suffering? Who reaches out to those who hide questions plaguing their souls—a problem of pain, the death of a friend, the fear of hell, the longing for intimacy? Soul work is a desperate cause. Those who suffer with doubts, shame, and fear often manifest their pain years later, mocking those who live with confident beliefs, or accosting the church for never reaching out. Many are tagged as enemies of the faith and rejected as troublemakers. They often become excellent atheists.

The quest for many is not merely for answers, but for that free country lying beyond the answers, where real questions and answers can be examined in the community of love. Apologetics has been most valuable in my life when it offered relief, allowing my hardest questions to bubble up from the center of my soul.

Doubts

Expressing doubt is a discipline in soul formation. It opens us to humility. Humility, the kind Jesus says children have (Matthew 18), is an attitude of considering yourself of little account. A posture of humility allows truth and knowledge to do their best work.

Every important question stems from some form of doubt, and when given voice, it helps the doubter carve a path to knowledge. Think of the questions of Nicodemus and Thomas, which drew some of the most popular lines from Jesus (John 3:4,9; 14:5; 20:25). We all live on the currency of doubters before us.

Jude 22 tells us to have mercy on those who doubt, because no one should be ashamed to admit she's lost. The shameful thing is refusing to be found. A real doubter takes the first step to owning her faith by exploring her questions. She knows that mimicking a creed or being told what to think will not alleviate her pain. She needs to see the answers woven into her journey and own them in her soul.

When I go into schools to speak to students for multiday events, I work with my wife to create a safe place for doubters. Most students will clam up or hide when asked to publically raise their hands and spout out questions. So we have them anonymously fill out three-by-five cards, all scribbling down their doubts together. I ask them, "Write your two most important questions in life, the ones that would make life easier for you if they were answered."

They bring their dark doubts out into the sunshine. Their questions have shown us that they long for goodness from a God they want to trust. Teacher and author Kathleen Norris shares about teaching poetry to fifth graders and finding one student's impressive poem called "My Very First Dad." It goes like this:

> I remember him
> like God in my heart…
> I remember his love,
> as big as Texas
> when I was born.[2]

Amazed, Norris asked about this young poet. The boy was the class troublemaker, below average academically, whose father deserted him the day he was born. Through a poetry assignment, the adults in his life learned about the size of the hole in his heart.

Like poetry, students' questions are windows into their souls. Ninety-nine percent of all the kids we address write down serious, soul-searching questions. I now have more than 7000 such questions accumulated from around the country—questions that draw my tears—silent suffering crying out from a quiet card.

My wife and I attempt to answer their questions conversationally and compassionately in a group setting. They hear what their peers struggle with and realize they are not alone. Some questions are simple, some more difficult. Last month one 12-year-old pulled me aside, lowered his voice and asked me, "Who made God?" In his humble but scared way, he said he hadn't yet received a good explanation to this question. Yet this deeply philosophical question was a whirlpool in his soul. He needed to know God was big enough to be trusted.

Some questions are more probing, like "Who created evil?" We have biblical stories of how evil began, but students want more. The question itself assumes a certain view of evil. And unless we have a solid knowledge of what evil is, we cannot answer the question of who created it.

The question seems solely intellectual at first, but it fits into a wider array of soul formation. If students can see that evil is a twisting of what is good, they will be more likely to understand that God's commands are clues to how we are made. "Why shouldn't we have sex before marriage?" students ask. They know God's commands, but that's not enough. Many assume that God makes rules, not according to nature, but according to His arbitrary desires. But when students see that sex before marriage twists the goodness of intimacy, they find an entirely different perspective of God. They see God as someone who is smart and who can be trusted. Once we see how evil twists our souls, we know better how to analyze it when temptation confronts us. "Why shouldn't I hang out with those kids?" Because my parents don't like them? Or because their ideas and lifestyles twist my soul? The second answer helps students map the world and find the knack to fit into it.[3]

In addition, most students (and adults too) have borrowed wrong assumptions for words we use every day. Words like faith, glory, sin, evil, law, love, truth. Misunderstanding these deep and meaningful ideas will keep our souls from flowing into abundant life. The motivation to do things for God's glory isn't very strong if we cannot explain what glory is.[4]

Other questions just have to be lived with the assurance that we are not alone. "What am I supposed to do with my life, you know, like, what is God's will?" "How do I stop being so depressed?" "Why did God take my mother when He knew I needed her?" Instead of spitting out Romans 8:28, we can offer companionship for the journey. Most Christian teens know these verses already. They long for a relational context—the fellowship of suffering. They want to know how you too have suffered in this. An apologist aims at soul formation when he focuses on questions he has wrestled with himself, giving a deeply personal touch, sharing as one passenger in life to another—soul to soul.

Apologetics Spotlights Diversions That Destroy Our Souls

Apologetics is always on the lookout for assaults on our faith. But some diversions fly under the radar. They twist our souls and keep us from freely and fully following Jesus.

I started to take a hard look at the multitude of diversions in my own life when my car stereo was stolen. When I picked up my Jeep from a repair shop, the stereo was gone. For six weeks I battled the insurance company for reimbursement. During that time, I found the silence a happy inconvenience. The first week without my stereo was bothersome. But after a time, something changed in me. I didn't feel restless driving without my music, and I had to admit—music had become a diversion for me, a drug I used to blanket the dissatisfaction in my soul.

We all live in a system willing to give you whatever diversion you need for your dissatisfaction. We can choose from consumerism, sex, busyness, food (or lack of), dating, fashion, cutting, spirituality, porn, celebrityism, sports, and voyeurism into the lives and thoughts of popular people (including not only those in Hollywood but also celebrity pastors and authors in the evangelical church). The Jedi mind tricks of marketing assure us this is normal and even expected in our society. Diversions rob us of peace, joy, and contentment, and they prevent us from developing disciplines like study, silence, and prayer. When we forget that diversions harm us, our souls pay a price.

Music, for example, is a gift from God, yet good gifts can be abused. In American culture, I believe the number one drug of choice is music. Not just secular music, but music, period. We've digitized it, distributed it, made complete concerts portable, and created our own soundtracks for our lives in the name of pleasure, moods, inspiration, or worship. But in young people's lives, an overdose of music can lead to soul-numbing dehumanization.

Speaking to teens, I often invite them to fast from their iPods and stereos. Try to go without any music for a day. Many groan, "Impossible!" Students tell me they don't know how they will live without their music. Music isn't the issue here; the problem is the soul's habit of avoiding real life.

Why the discipline? Diversions dull and disconnect us from everyday life, where God is at work in us. When diversions become addictions, they disconnect us from ourselves, our thoughts, our ideas, our growing up, our dreams, and what God thinks of us. We let them disconnect us because we often think diversions are not a soul issue. I've seen teens disengage from their communities, be they in Los Angeles or rural Colorado, because they doubt that their local church, school, friends, or family have anything to offer. They think they are better informed by the bands they identify with. I've talked with college students who believe that the new, trendy thing is the right thing. I've engaged with adults susceptible to designer spirituality because it fits their schedule and their needs, not because they find a more powerful god who will bring them a good life. The hungry, the shamed, the inadequate, the lost—these souls latch onto diversion, clinging to these security blankets, because they believe diversions bring a greater hope for their restlessness than does the gospel.

God made humans with various differences and creative abilities for a reason: not so we would follow every new pop-culture idea, but so each of us would bear His image in the unique ways we can.

Apologetics gives an answer. Aware of culture and ideas that potentially hurt us, apologetics uncovers diversions that challenge our faith. It protects churches from adding to the diversions and seeks ways to foster spiritual growth. In places I've challenged teens to unplug, I've invariably gotten e-mails from those who've taken the challenge. It's awakened their creativity. They write songs, tell stories, seek out counselors, and explore new vocations. As spiritual health begins to blossom, reason and imagination link hands. Apologetics for the next generation is a voice in the wilderness, calling out for the freedom of humanity.

Apologetics Fosters Love and Conversation in Community

We need each other—all of us. For too long apologetics has been perceived as an impersonal and intolerant opportunity for one-upmanship. Our way forward in apologetics is to open up others to love, to lift their eyes to the hills, to find out where their help comes from. What if, instead of impersonally stating that alternative worldviews are false, we spoke about ways that other religions personally degrade us as humans? Look at the way the Eastern religions demoralize their adherents. Hinduism says the untouchables are less valuable than others because of bad karma. Buddhism says we need to grow beyond being human into the enlightened state that absorbs our unique personalities, disintegrating our desires into the One. Or look at shame-based religions like Islam (some of this sickness still lives in Christianity too) that motivate with fear and guilt rather than love, acceptance, and freedom. Or look at atheism: Human value is measured by the degree of functionality of each individual.

We cannot build a real community of love—the kind the soul needs—out of that. Sharing our faith, defending our faith, includes making truth claims but also moves into human claims. I need my neighbor to know the truth better, even a Christian neighbor, so he can be a healthy human and watch my back from the diversions and false beliefs I hold. Healthy humans love the triune God of love and engage souls through conversation, presence, and love. Apologetics can make this happen. I love with truth so I can in turn be loved this way. We are neighbors who love neighbors and together love God.

I am active in an off-roading community. Through trail rides and online forums, I connect with people I would never meet otherwise. Last month, one of my friends turned his life to Jesus. He shared how a mutual Jeep friend connected with him. "And you had a part in this too, you know," he said, surprising me and my wife. "Yes, when we spent time together on the trail, I noticed you guys didn't talk and act like the typical twenty- and thirty-somethings I know. You talked differently. I wanted what you had." I told him that when getting to know people, I often don't talk about Jesus for a while because I want us to get to know each other as people. He added, "Had you been overt about Jesus, I would have been turned off and missed the life that you shared."

Loving people for their own sake is not only a gospel discipline to build our souls but is likely the best strategy for finding the neighborly love we want and the neighborly love we need in return.

Conclusion

When we take a humanitarian apologetic seriously, we will see it not just as a trend or a method. Rather it is an invitation into a lifestyle of seeing, knowing, and loving the sheer goodness and meaning of being a healthy, loving human. It tills our souls. It opens us to God and a wider world.

Dale Fincher is the author of *Living with Questions* and cofounder of the husband/wife Soulation team.

Part 2

NEW METHODS

This past weekend I was at a conference along some of my heroes in life, including James Dobson, Charles Colson, Lee Strobel, Hank Hanegraaff, and my own father, Josh McDowell. Like the men of Issachar, these men understood the times and knew what to do (1 Chronicles 12:32). They are significant leaders of today, and their influence will continue to linger indefinitely.

But times are changing. The new millennium is bringing fresh challenges in all aspects of life. While those who have come before us provide immeasurable wisdom, we need to be willing to step outside the box and take risks for the sake of advancing the kingdom of God. We must wrestle with questions like these: How do we creatively capture people's attention so they will entertain the truth of Christ? How important are stories in reaching this new generation? How do we introduce a generation of young people, who have experienced broken and shattered relationships, to a relationship with Jesus?

These are critical questions that every minister today must effectively engage. Yet these are only a few of the issues discussed in this section. The bottom line is this: Apologetics for a new generation must be more concerned about winning people than winning arguments. If you have an open mind and a willing heart, each of these writers will lead you down a trail that could lead to a transformation of your ministry. They will help you to wrestle with creative and practical means for reaching a new generation. Are you ready to go?

Sean McDowell

CAPTURING THE IMAGINATION BEFORE ENGAGING THE MIND

by Craig J. Hazen

vividly remember a short play I watched in a church one evening many years ago when I was in my early twenties. I had been a Christian for only a short time and had begun reading works in Christian apologetics that were recommended to me by theologically astute friends. The play dealt with a theme in Christian apologetics, and although I can't recall the titles or content of books I was reading at the time, I definitely remember the play.

Five or six men dressed in bedraggled New Testament–era clothing were sitting around a campfire, warming themselves and speaking to one another in hushed voices. The faux first-century campfire dialogue had to do with a group of the apostles of Jesus Christ cooking up a story and colluding with one another about what they would tell the world concerning the identity, death, and supposed miracles and resurrection of Jesus. The dialogue among the actors that night went something like this:

> There is nothing ridiculous in dying for nothing at all. And why should we dislike for no good reason undergoing scourging and bodily torture, and if need be to experience imprisonment, dishonor, and insult for what is untrue? Let us now make this our business. We will tell the same falsehoods, and invent stories that will benefit nobody, neither ourselves, nor those we deceive, nor him who is deified by our lies.

> None of us must fail in zeal, for it is no petty contest that we dare, and no common prizes lie before us—but most likely the punishments inflicted according to the laws of each land. We will face bonds, of course, torture, imprisonment, fire and sword, and wild beasts. We must greet them all with enthusiasm, and meet evil bravely, having our Master as our model. For what could be finer than to make both gods and men our enemies for no reason at all, and to have no enjoyment of any kind, to have no profit of our dear ones, to make no money, to have no hope of anything good at all, but just to be deceived and to deceive without aim or object?

The reason the play stayed with me all these years is because it so effectively made a crucial apologetic point. Skeptics sometimes bring up the objection that the closest followers of Jesus probably made up the miracle stories and the account of the resurrection, but this dramatic presentation demonstrates in an unforgettable way just how ludicrous that idea is. Why would any of these "deceivers" face tremendous loss and death to maintain a lie that didn't benefit them, their families, or their friends whatsoever? Well, they wouldn't. And seeing this acted out by an amateur troupe did more to lodge this in my understanding than the writing of any heavyweight apologist I was reading at the time.

This story has one other interesting aspect. The actors probably told the audience about it at the time, but it didn't sink in for me until later. This dialogue was very ancient—probably written before AD 311—and authored by one of the top thinkers and historians from the earliest church, Eusebius of Caesarea.[1] And Eusebius was by no means the first to use this effective technique.

Using creative elements to hammer home an important apologetic point is as old as the gospel itself. Although Jesus was not normally engaged in what we call apologetics, He was certainly an amazing trendsetter in illustrating His points with pithy, memorable stories. How many books have been written around the globe and through the centuries analyzing Jesus' parables—and not just interpreting the content of the parables but also analyzing why His parables are so memorable and effective? Jesus was obviously tapping into something very deep and powerful in the human soul when He used stories to communicate the great truths of the kingdom. Those who are called to defend the faith in this generation would do well to pay attention to Jesus (in a preeminent way, of course) as well as other successful storytellers as they use narratives to connect with their hearers and readers and carry them to conclusions about the most important issues in life—including the truth of the gospel and the Christian view of the world.

The Tough Minded and the Tender Minded

Apologists most frequently use rational and evidential argumentation to demonstrate and reinforce the truths of Scripture. I personally have an inclination toward this kind of discourse. Arguments presented in this way were very influential on me and my coming to love God with all my mind. However, not everyone, indeed probably not most people, are moved toward religious truth in this way. Indeed, my old teacher John Warwick Montgomery divided the audience for apologetics into two basic groups. The first he called the "tough minded"—those who found logic, propositional argument, and hard evidence to be very persuasive. The second group he called the "tender minded"—those who are persuaded more by artistic, subjective, and emotional vehicles than by strict rational argument. Of course he had various gradations in these categories, but he thought different approaches were warranted if you could get a fix on your listener's personality. The idea here is parallel to the apostle Paul's methodology: "I have become all things to all men, so that I may by all means save some" (1 Corinthians 9:22).

Deep Myths and Archetypes

In practical terms, Montgomery never did much more than sketch out what a tender-minded approach to apologetics might look like. He left that to great modern exemplars of this method like C.S. Lewis and J.R.R. Tolkien. However, Montgomery and others did attempt to articulate why this tender-minded approach was important and effective—it has a substantial theoretical base. In getting at the connection between imagination and apologetics in the service of the gospel, I think a brief review of this might be helpful.

Carl Gustav Jung, the great Swiss psychoanalyst of the twentieth century, compared the dream lives of his patients with the perennial symbols created by human cultures throughout the ages and found a set of images that seemed to capture the basic themes of human experience and universal human need. Jung ended up rejecting Sigmund Freud's reductionistic materialism, so he was able to identify the existence of a common psychic life among all people through history that he called the "archetypes of the collective unconscious." Of course, Jung, coming from the field of psychoanalysis, was not the only one to identify these universal symbolic patterns that bubble up among people everywhere. Specialists in areas of study such as myth and folklore (Lucien Lévy-Bruhl, Joseph Campbell, Stith Thompson, Clyde Kluckhohn), religious studies (Mircea Eliade, Henri Hubert, Marcel Mauss), and anthropology (Claude Lévi-Strauss) have also identified these symbolic archetypes. Images such as the Wise Old Man, Earth Mother, the Persona, the Hero, and the Witch or Trickster all denote in a transcultural way various aspects of human drama and psychic life.

Montgomery illustrated this by using one of the most familiar fairy-tale formulas known by most of us in Western culture because of Mother Goose and Disney animation.

> In the common folktale of "Sleeping Beauty," a Princess is put into a deathlike trance by the machinations of an evil Witch; impenetrable brambles grow up around the Princess's castle; and all is restored only when, in fulfillment of a prophecy, a Prince comes and raises her up with the kiss of love; this is followed by a marriage feast and the declaration that "they lived happily ever after."[2]

The archetypes are striking in this story for those of us who affirm the Christian view of the world. The princess represents the human race fallen and is unable to save herself. The witch (the devil) wants to destroy this beauty, who is adored by the king (God the Father). The prince (a savior) is driven by love to overcome the brambles and barriers to reach the fallen princess. The prince's kiss raises the princess to happiness evermore. We know this story well. But so do other cultures who have never heard of Sleeping Beauty, Mother Goose, or Disney. The names for the characters might be different, but the archetypal roles they play are not. Are there certain basic characters, themes, and stories built into all of us in some way? Given the pervasive evidence, this appears to be the case. But an even more specific conclusion might be warranted. The basic gospel story itself might very well be imprinted on us at some sublevel of awareness.

The famous twentieth-century Christian author and scholar J.R.R. Tolkien took time to reflect not only on his own fiction writings but also on the culmination of the timeless myths and folktales of the past in relation to the Gospels.

> The Gospels contain…a story of a larger kind which embraces all the essence of fairy stories. They contain many marvels— peculiarly artistic, beautiful, and moving; "mythical" in their perfect, self-contained significance; and at the same time powerfully symbolic and allegorical; and among the marvels is the greatest and most complete conceivable eucatastrophe [happy ending]. The Birth of Christ is the eucatastrophe of Man's history. The Resurrection is the eucatastrophe of the story of the Incarnation. This story begins and ends in joy. It has pre-eminently the "inner consistency of reality." There is no tale ever told that men would rather find was true, and none which so many sceptical men have accepted as true on its own merits. For the Art of it has the supremely convincing tone of Primary Art, that is, of Creation. To reject it leads either to sadness or to wrath…Because this story is supreme; and it is true. Art has been verified: God is the Lord, of the angels, and of men—and of elves. Legend and History have met and fused.[3]

Tolkien's friend C.S. Lewis came to a similar conclusion in his essay "Myth Became Fact":

> The heart of Christianity is myth which is also a fact. The old myth of the Dying God, *without ceasing to be myth,* comes down from the heaven of legend and imagination to the earth of history. It *happens*—at a particular date, in a particular place, followed by definable historical consequences.

The timeless formula that we have come to know with regard to folktales is that they begin with "once upon a time" and end with "and they lived happily ever after." Each of us appears to have a deep and not-so-subtle longing to reach this end, but we are trapped and in need of a prince from outside our castle-prison to storm the walls and to set us free. In the case of the Christian faith, the great myth has been realized. We no longer look to the ever-indefinite "once upon a time." Rather, we see the myth become reality in knowable time and space. The New Testament writer Luke began his record of the greatest story ever told by fixing it firmly in history: "Now in those days a decree went out from Caesar Augustus, that a census be taken of all the inhabited earth. This was the first census taken while Quirinius was governor of Syria" (2:1-2). Or as the apostle John wrote, "The Word became flesh and made his dwelling among us. We have seen his glory, the glory of the One and Only, who came from the Father, full of grace and truth" (John 1:14 NIV). The great myth, that which seems too good to be true, has become part of history. It is *our* story.

If it is true that the combined weight of collective dream life, visionary encounters, and the great myths and stories emerging from human experience point toward a deeper story that captures our problem and the solution at the most fundamental level, then it is not surprising to hear some of the greatest thinkers in human history say, along with Saint Augustine, "Thou hast made us for thyself, O Lord, and our hearts are restless until they rest in thee."

I would consider this the essential reason why the tender-minded approach cannot be neglected even when dealing with tough-minded skeptics. We are tapping into something that we know is imprinted on each individual at some level and that can be used powerfully by the Holy Spirit to move everyone's heart and mind in the right direction.

The Power of Imaginative Expression

Apart from this grand and powerful theory regarding some inherent human archetypes and stories, other more practical issues make appeals to the imagination a potent apologetic tool. Madison Avenue advertising agencies help companies make billions of dollars every year by creating images that communicate more persuasively than any philosopher's loquacious argument ever could. Hollywood producers create trends and alter the way people think about important issues by wrapping their views on reality and ethics inside of compelling stories, and over the long haul, these are effective at moving public opinion on these matters. The theologian Alister McGrath put it this way:

> Argument will always have a place in Christian apologetics. But it urgently needs to be supplemented by an appeal to imagery. "Imagination is not to be divorced from the facts; it is a way of illuminating the facts" (A.N. Whitehead). Arguments are precise; images are suggestive. We need to meditate on those remarkable words of some Greeks who came to Philip: "Sir, we wish to see Jesus" (John 12:21). Here is our task: to help people see Jesus Christ with their own eyes. Let us learn from Christ, who opened his parables, not with a definition ("The kingdom of God *is*…"), but with an image ("The kingdom of God *is like*…"). The parables themselves are remarkably effective in inviting their hearers to step inside their narrative worlds and in stirring the imagination. The parables excite; too often, arguments dull.[4]

I guess a picture really is worth at least a thousand words, and a word-picture or story is the next best thing to an actual visual. As Douglas Wilson put it, we need to learn to "know poetically" and, of course, to communicate poetically as well. He meant by this that perfect reasoning belongs only to God. Given our finitude, we will always depend on the metaphorical to explain great truths and make connections with our audience. Therefore, we should do our best to maximize our metaphorical impact. However, we are always in danger of doing bad poetry or creating impoverished metaphor.

> The Bible compares God to very mundane things, but does so with poetic wonder. God "shall come down like rain upon the mown grass; as showers that water the earth" (Ps. 72:6). If someone were to claim that the forgiveness of Christ clears the head like a really good nasal spray, the problem is one of a tin ear, and *not* the introduction of noses into the discussion of spiritual things.[5]

We should certainly recognize the danger, but it should not dissuade us. I have no doubt that many true disciples of the Lord Jesus Christ have anything but a tin ear. I have contact regularly with brilliant novelists, musicians, painters, composers, sculptors, directors, screenwriters, actors, and essayists among the saints of God who have not entertained in a serious way how their creative impulses could best serve Christ and His kingdom.

We seem to lack a tradition of imaginative expression in the evangelical churches, so those with high-level talents aren't sure how they fit in or where. I am no fan of the way evangelical postmoderns (some of whom identify with the Emergent church movement) handle the traditional claims of moral and theological knowledge (they can tend toward relativism and pluralism—sometimes without knowing it or without knowing the ramifications). But one aspect of this movement has shown promise: They seem much more adept at making a place for avant-garde forms of creative expression through art, music, film, and so on. Of course, without a solid understanding and grounding in knowledge and truth, this emergent creative expression does not stand much of a chance of assisting the essential task of apologetics in our generation, or for that matter, assisting the proclamation of the gospel itself!

The great challenge today seems to be to find a way to allow serious Christian artistic, literary, and musical expression to flourish without diluting or altering the essential truths of Scripture. If this fusion can come forward in a robust way, the benefits for the kingdom will be immense and longstanding. So how do we do it?

To set a course for an energized synthesis of imagination and truth, we need not reinvent the wheel. Indeed, the very best engineers have tinkered with this wheel over the centuries so that it spins truer than ever. Eusebius, Lewis, Tolkien, Handel, Michelangelo, Milton, Rossetti, and Paley have already shown us the way to have perennial impact.

When integrating the imagination with the basic tasks of apologetics, what can we learn from the past masters? What special adjustments do we need to make for the peculiarities of our own time and place? I will offer a few morsels here.

Knowing the Primordial Story Intimately

As Christians we are in possession of the key to God's grand designs and to our place in the great drama. Know it well. It can be summed up in three (very rich and weighty) words: creation, fall, and redemption. Because we have access to the Scriptures, we have a distinct advantage over the world. We know key secrets about how the story begins, the central conflict, and most importantly, the ending. We have been able to read the conclusion before everyone else, so we can make decisions about how to proceed with real knowledge. Not only that, but we know our fellow travelers well. From the standpoint of Scripture we can peer into the human psyche like no one else. We certainly don't have all the answers, but we have deeper and more profound clues about what motivates people, what sin has done to us, what people are seeking, and what they long for to fill the vacuum in their souls.

Remember the Goal

We are attempting to fuse the imagination and the apologetic endeavor for a reason, and we must keep that reason in front of us.

We want to connect with people where they are and move them toward the cross of Christ. Alister McGrath said it this way: "Good apologetics is…a creative imaginative appeal to what your audience already knows, in order to get them interested in, even excited about, what they have yet to discover."[6] We want to produce and use apologetic tools that effectively clear the brush and make an unencumbered path to the saving presence of God. The apostle Paul wrote about this task: "The weapons we fight with…have divine power to demolish strongholds. We demolish arguments and every pretension that sets itself up against the knowledge of God." Our arguments and creative connections thus become powerful tools for the Holy Spirit to use in tearing down the barriers that keep people from faith.

The Creative Product Has to Be Good

High-quality art doesn't always make you feel happy. Even dark music, visuals, and screenplays can move people in God's direction. Consider the film *The Exorcism of Emily Rose* (2005) for example. It was startlingly frightening at certain points. But it was written and directed by a thoughtful Christian, Scott Derrickson, who used the horror genre to point intentionally toward a true nonphysical reality among us: demonic powers. Even films about bad things such as drugs, prostitution, and traitorous behavior can be good if they show the true consequences of sinful behavior. I remember years ago seeing a spy movie called *The Falcon and the Snowman* (1985), which captured the deep personal pain of getting too far into illegal activities. The movie would have been a great antidote for anyone contemplating criminal activity. It was good in that it was real—it did not whitewash the results of sin.

Let me address "good" briefly from another angle. Both of the films mentioned above were good in another sense. The stories captured people's attention, and the technical proficiency matched the standards of the profession. That is "good" used in the same way that people use it when recommending a movie they like to a friend. "It was good, you really should see it." In order for our creative products to be impactful, they must meet this standard. However, here is an important caveat. I did not say a film or book or composition needs to be great or classic. I say this so that we do not get dissuaded in attempting these important creative works. You are not likely to be the next C.S. Lewis, but if you have gifting or desire to express truths that reflect parts of the gospel, you should give it a try. It is risky, but as Alister McGrath concluded, "Happily, the rewards often enormously outweigh those risks. They are profoundly worth taking."[7]

Don't Wear the Gospel on Your Sleeve

One huge advantage of articulating Christian ideas in creative new ways is that you have a chance to avoid stereotypes that often shut down unbelievers' attraction to the things of God. Many thousands of people responded to the gospel message at Billy Graham crusades. But we forget that many, many more don't respond, or worse, would never dream of darkening the door of an arena holding such an event. The evangelistic formulas and images we use most often are easily recognized by unbelievers, and those people generally react by turning away. The creative arts have the power to draw unbelievers in and give them a fresh view of what the gospel means beyond the stereotypical ideas they have been clinging to for years.

If you are writing a novel or screenplay, find a couple compelling elements of the Christian worldview to weave into the story. Use a side door to introduce and unpack these elements. Put the most profound comments in the mouths of unbelievers or those who would not be considered pristine Christian heroes. Have discoveries about true eternal things made in unusual ways by characters the reader would not expect. Break the stereotypes, avoid the formulas, and be creative.

Have Something to Say

In my view, this is the most difficult of my suggestions because it requires a lot of hard work beyond the creative craft that you might love. We need to have something to say, and the more timeless, the more salient, the more penetrating, the better. There is only one way to have something to say that meets criteria like these, and that is to read, hear, view, and experience the greatest works and ideas that have come down through the ages.

There is a reason that C.S. Lewis's Chronicles of Narnia have moved people at many different levels for several generations—Lewis had a lot to say. Everyone over 20 years old knows that these are not just children's stories meant to entertain, although they accomplish that with great flair. Because Lewis knew the intellectual controversies of his own day, he was able to address them in creative ways, not only in his erudite essays but also in his children's stories. In *The Silver Chair*, Lewis incorporated a marvelous refutation of a philosopher named Ludwig Feuerbach who had helped set the stage for the atheism of Sigmund Freud and Karl Marx. Using a dialogue between a witch, a prince, and a couple of children, and calling upon a little backstage help from Plato, Lewis shows the absurd nature of Feuerbach's idea that God is not real, but rather a projection of our deepest desires. This would not have been possible for Lewis had he not had familiarity with intellectual controversies in his own day and a knowledge of timeless ideas through thinkers such as Plato.

I am not saying we all need to go out and do graduate work in classics or philosophy. Mastering some key ideas to incorporate into creative works of Christian apologetics is not as daunting as it might seem. Anytime I feel as if I don't have anything to say, I start to read the works of some excellent thinkers—whether they be contemporaries or classical. I am always amazed how stimulating it is; how ideas and new conceptual connections come flooding in.

If you have creative gifts and a passion for Christ and for lost people, and if you are willing to drink deeply at the well of timeless Christian knowledge, the impact of your fresh apologetic work will be felt far and wide—perhaps for generations to come. We need you to go for it.

Craig J. Hazen is the founder and director of the master of arts program in Christian apologetics at Biola University, the editor of *Philosophia Christi*, and author of *Five Sacred Crossings*.

CONVERSATIONAL APOLOGETICS: EVANGELISM FOR THE NEW MILLENNIUM

by David Geisler

G rowing up as the son of a well-known Christian apologist afforded me some advantages from an early age, including an opportunity to peek into this window of Christian apologetics. I don't remember struggling much or having many doubts about the Christian faith, even as a child. As a young boy of 12, I was more interested in something else: how I could witness to my friends and classmates. Deep down inside, I just knew that if I was serious about being a disciple of Christ, I needed to do something to reach others with the gospel.

Having some background in apologetic issues and a passion for evangelism has provided me a unique platform to observe and critique both disciplines. It has also provided me opportunities to practice both disciplines in a complementary way. That is why I am bothered when apologists and evangelists don't seem to speak the same language or even understand the value that each side could contribute in our united witness to others. I am troubled that far too many of those who are skilled in the area of Christian apologetics don't seem to have a deep burden for reaching the lost. Yet some of those who do have a great heart and passion for the lost don't seem particularly interested in growing in their knowledge of apologetic issues! I feel bad when I walk into a Christian bookstore and see many good books on apologetics and many good books on evangelism, but very few on how to actually use apologetics more practically in evangelism.[1] I sometimes sense a lack of appreciation on each side as to the important insights that each could contribute in our combined witness to others.

From my perspective, each side has been culpable in some ways. I had a conversation with a well-known and respected evangelist who tried to assure me that God had called him to simply proclaim the gospel, so he didn't feel a need to concern himself with answering questions that others may have about the Christian faith and thus engage others in apologetic dialogue. The gospel may be simple in some ways, but getting to the gospel is not always so simple in our world. I was puzzled that this seemed to escape his notice.

I also have difficulty understanding how some evangelists and Christian leaders can consider that the objective elements to our faith are not that important in our witness to others. Anyone who reads 1 Corinthians 15 cannot escape the fact that the apostle Paul considered some kind of objectivity to our faith as Christians so critical that if someone could show us that we are wrong about Jesus, we were instructed to renounce our faith and consider ourselves to be "of all men most to be pitied" (1 Corinthians 15:19).

In today's world, everyone seems to have a religious experience of some sort. How are we to determine which are legitimate, if any? In such a world, a strictly testimonial approach to evangelism seems incomplete. Here is the question: How do we effectively share the gospel in today's world, where right and wrong are seen as matters of personal preference like ice cream flavors? If people have no sense of their own sinfulness, why would they need a savior?[2] Our world believes no one religious experience is more valid than another, and therefore no one "story" should be preferred over any other. Clearly, apologetics is needed.

And some apologists I know could learn a few things from evangelists. Apologists need to learn that sometimes people are so spiritually blinded from the truth that we can't even reason with them initially about what they believe and why (Ephesians 4:18). Instead we need to pray that the Holy Spirit will open their eyes and ears to see and hear what we are saying about Christ and thus be open to embracing Him (2 Corinthians 4:3-6).

Apologists also need to attend to the fine art of listening and speaking in such a way that others will be more open to really hear what we have to say about Jesus. How we say things matters as much as what we say. Unfortunately, far too many apologists have not developed a greater sensitivity as to how to present the truth of the gospel and also an ability to gauge when it might be appropriate or not appropriate to do so.

Using Apologetics in Constructive Ways

The apologetic task has become more difficult in this new generation, especially when so many Christians have difficulty understanding how useful it can be in our daily witness. For some, this may have something to do with not knowing how to use apologetics in appropriate ways without attacking the person in the process! Unfortunately, it is all too common to stereotype apologists as type-A personalities who like to argue with people and who may be perceived as a little insensitive in their dialogue. Certainly as Christians we must find a way to be faithful to the scriptural mandates to "destroy speculation" (2 Corinthians 10:5), and yet we must do so in a way that others will know that we deeply love and care about them (1 Corinthians 13:2-3; 1 Thessalonians 2:8). This is an art that we need to master to be faithful to the commands of Scripture and to do so in a way that does not come across as harsh or insensitive.

We must also be careful not to come across as arrogant or portray ourselves as being better than others because of our beliefs. As others have often said, Christianity really is one beggar telling another beggar where he found bread. If we are going to be heard, we must learn to present the truth of Christ in a meek and gentle way. We certainly should never speak the truth in order to score notches on our spiritual belts.

Moreover, as apologists we must go the extra mile in talking with others. For example, whenever I share the gospel with a prebeliever, I always try to temper my approach with an open disposition. When prebelievers ask me questions like, "Is it possible you could be wrong about Christ?" I will simply say something like, "Hey, if I'm wrong, please tell me, because I don't want to believe a lie." Remember, even the Bereans went on a fact-checking quest in order to see if what Paul was saying was true (Acts 17:11).

Furthermore, it is important to demonstrate a teachable spirit and an openness to learn. Otherwise we may alienate people and cut off any spiritual dialogue prematurely. It also may help us to be more honest with ourselves about what theological beliefs we should hold on to tightly and those that may be considered more or less gray areas. The apostle Paul himself reminds us that we don't see everything in this life so clearly (1 Corinthians 13:12). We should always be open to humbly reflecting on our beliefs.

Making It Practical

One of the biggest reasons why many Christians don't see the value of apologetics in our witness to others is that very few have been taught how to use it in practical ways that actually produce results. Some may even see this exercise of engaging others in apologetic dialogue as futile. Certainly this is understandable when so many Christians have used apologetics primarily as a bat to whack people over the head with truth and deconstruct (dismantle) their beliefs. I find that in living in a post-Christian world, many people are turned off by the deconstruction of their religious beliefs by their zealous Christians friends. We must do more to reach people than simply tear down their arguments (2 Corinthians 10:5). People can quickly get defensive, even in casual conversations that happen to touch directly on spiritual matters or have indirect spiritual implications.[3] You may lose the chance to continue the conversations, especially if you have already put people on the defensive.

If we are going to make some progress in today's world, we need to balance our efforts better in using apologetics appropriately in evangelism. But we must proceed with caution. We need an apologetic that we can live with that will help us stand against the tide of relativism, and yet one that is sensitive enough to speak to the concerns and priorities of our unsaved postmodern friends.[4] Consider some practical suggestions.

Allow Others to Surface the Truth for Themselves

In today's world, allowing others to surface the truth themselves is usually more effective than proclaiming the truth as we have done for so long. Thus, when we use apologetics in our evangelism, we need to avoid preaching at others or arguing with them. Rather, we can invite them to join us on a spiritual journey in which they can explore their beliefs and learn more about Jesus. Many times, this can be accomplished simply by asking thought-provoking questions.

For example, one day I had a conversation with someone in the exercise room where I was working out. Let's just call him John. I was trying to remember where our previous conversation ended. To refresh my memory I asked him, "What church did you say you were going to?"

He replied that he goes to such-and-such Catholic church, paused for a brief moment, and then added, "We believe in Mary."

For clarification I asked him, "What do you mean by, 'We believe in Mary'?"

He took a few minutes and stumbled over his words but finally said something to the effect that Mary makes up for the part that Jesus lacks. I could have pointed out that the Bible does not teach this, but I knew that saying this so directly would make him defensive, so I allowed him to surface the truth for himself by asking him thought-provoking questions. "But do you know what 1 Timothy 2:5 says? 'There is one God, and one mediator also between God and men, the man Christ Jesus.' What do you think this verse teaches?" He seemed unsure so I further asked, "Doesn't this verse teach that Jesus is the only mediator who can atone for mankind's sins?" He reluctantly agreed. I further added, "Certainly I can see how some Catholics could see Mary as being a helpful person who could pray for them, just as some Baptist might consider it helpful if they got Billy Graham to pray for them. But can Mary do anything to help you atone for your sins in any way?"

He thought about it for a moment and finally said to me, "No, she cannot." Certainly his reaction may not have been so positive had I not taken the time to help him surface the truth for himself.

Build Heart Bridges to the Cross

Using apologetics to deconstruct someone's false beliefs may not be very effective unless we also build positive heart bridges to the cross. A heart bridge may be a deep-seated need that only Jesus can meet fully. Solomon alludes to this need when he declares that "He has also set eternity in the hearts of men; yet they cannot fathom what God has done from the beginning to end" (Ecclesiastes 3:11 NIV). For effective witness to new generations, one must balance deconstructive and heart-bridge-building approaches. If our questions come across as though we are attempting to load both barrels of our shotgun, we should not be surprised when people decide not to (figuratively speaking) come to our hunting party, especially when they may suspect that they are the target! They may not even be curious enough to want to find a resolution to the inconsistencies in their own beliefs.[5]

Certainly we need to help people discover not only the bad news about the human condition but also the good news of the cross. One day I was talking to a Chinese lady in Singapore. For ten or fifteen minutes, I listened to her talk about how great Buddhism is. Eventually, I just asked her one simple question, "As a mother, don't you desire good things for your children?" This one statement seemed to catch her by surprise because it left her speechless. On some level she must have realized that a true Buddhist is not supposed to desire anything.[6] Having gotten her attention, I asked one other simple question: "Do you know what Jesus taught about desire? The answer to man's problem is not to give up on desire, but to have the right desire. Christians believe that when we invite Christ to come into our life, He changes us from the inside out so we no longer desire to do the bad things; instead, we desire to do the good things that He wants us to do."

She was open to hear my question because I listened to her patiently and earned the right to be heard. But also it was because I coupled a discrepancy in her belief system with a question that built a heart bridge. By coupling those two things I was essentially saying to her, "I know you have difficulty with living without any desire. But the good news is that Jesus has an answer for desire going amok. Would you like to hear what it is?"

By coupling her uncertainty with a positive heart bridge, I was also keeping in mind the three *D*s taught in our *Conversational Evangelism* approach: We must ask questions in a way that surfaces Doubt (uncertainty), minimizes Defensiveness, and creates a Desire (curiosity) to hear more.[7] I have found that using probing questions with the three Ds in mind can play a significant part in creating greater willingness not only to hear more about Jesus but also to make a decision to trust in Christ! The bottom line is, remember that people may not be motivated to get out of a leaky boat unless you can provide them with a better boat to get into. As a result we must do more than just use apologetics to deconstruct someone's false beliefs. Certainly, like good doctors, we must do more than just diagnose their illness correctly. We must provide the right treatment as well!

Apologetics Lite

In the current cultural climate, a light approach to apologetics is most effective in our dialogue with others. We need to give prebelievers just enough information for them to notice differences between Jesus and other religious teachers and to want to hear more. With "apologetics lite," the biggest intellectual obstacles surface quickly. If none arise, you don't have to address nonissues. We certainly don't want to pepper listeners with so much evidence that they feel defensive and obligated to attack our beliefs in return.

Light apologetics can also help prebelievers feel more comfortable with us until we surface their real barriers to Christ, which are not always intellectual. Jeremiah 17:9 says, "The heart is more deceitful than all else and is desperately sick; who can know it?" Sometimes the heart keeps us from accepting the truth. We need to uncover these hidden barriers to the cross.[8]

One approach I have is to ask prebelievers simple questions. "I'm curious—how does Jesus fit into your religious beliefs?" It's amazing how many people have never been asked this question. Yet it's a great way to encourage people to think more seriously about Jesus without making them feel defensive.

Of course, some people may not buy into what we are saying. That's when a deeper apologetic may be more helpful. However, we must be careful not to engage people on a deeper level intellectually if we have already determined that they are more interested in arguing with us and proving us wrong. Certainly we have better things to do with our time than to argue with people who are not willing to openly discuss the claims of Christ and the evidence to substantiate those claims.

Find Agreement Even in Our Disagreements

Find common agreement even in your disagreements with those you are trying to reach (Acts 17:22). If you come across as someone who is not open to seeing the truth in another's perspective, you can be seen as intolerant or narrow-minded, and right away you'll lose your credibility as a witness. The fact is, we can find some truth we can agree on (though it may be very small) in every worldview. For example, when a pluralist claims that all religions are the same, we can say, "Certainly I would agree that there are some things that all religions believe in, like caring for others and being kind," yet we should also point out that some important differences make them distinct. We should also remember that we are able to find these points of agreement with those we have strong disagreements with, because God has given mankind some understanding of the world from creation and from the moral law He has written on the heart (Romans

1:20; 2:14-15). This may take some effort, but if we dig deep enough we will find them because even worldviews that are totally opposed to Christianity use objective truth to affirm their beliefs.

The Practical Benefit of Changing Our Approach

Conversational apologetics broadens the goal of our conversations. The idea is to dialogue with others in such a way that they want to hear more about our Jesus or at least to continue the spiritual conversation later. Unfortunately, many of us don't make this the focus of our conversations with others, so we miss important bridge-building moments because we have been taught a narrow view of evangelism. Many of us have been taught to share as much of the content of the gospel with as many people as we can in the shortest period possible. This is not a biblical approach. Sometimes we sow seeds, and sometimes we help reap the harvest. We can't reap all the time. If we aren't careful when we share with people, we will close the door to further conversations. We may even accidentally prevent other Christians from joining the conversation in the future.

Our goal should be to talk to people in such a way today that the next time they see us, they are eager to continue the spiritual conversation, not run the other direction! We will be more likely to reach our ultimate goal if we plant a seed today, water it tomorrow, and look for the fruit after a season (1 Corinthians 3:6).

Saying everything we want to say to our friends about Jesus in a short period of time is usually counterproductive. Jesus Himself demonstrated this conviction when He told His disciples in John 16:12, "I have many more things to say to you, but you cannot bear them now." Certainly prudence dictates that we should be careful not only in what we say to our friends but also in what we don't say, especially when they may not be ready to hear it yet. I find that when I take a longer approach in sharing the gospel with others, they end up with a better understanding about the gospel. Also, they are either closer to making decisions for Christ or at least clearer about the issues that are holding them back.

Conclusion

Clearly, we need to develop a greater feel for what is an appropriate use of apologetics in our witness on a daily basis if we are going to make a real difference in this new generation. We need to remember that engaging others in pre-evangelism conversations is more of an art than a science, and is certainly, like discipleship, more caught than taught. Simply knowing these principles will not guarantee success. We need to go out and put these principles into practice. We will certainly make mistakes, but perhaps we will learn from those mistakes and be more effective the next time we engage others on spiritual matters. May God help us to better understand the times in which we live and, like the men of Issachar, know then what we should do (1 Chronicles 12:32).

Dr. David Geisler is the founder and president of Meekness and Truth Ministries in Singapore and coauthor of *Conversational Evangelism*.

AN INTERVIEW WITH GREG STIER

Sean McDowell: What topics in apologetics seem to be especially relevant and important to this generation of young people?

Greg Stier:

What are the evidences for the existence of a higher power?
Why is there evil in the world?
Can all religions be right?
Who is Jesus?
Is the Bible reliable?
What is truth, and can I know it with certainty?

Sean: Do we need to make substantial changes in our approach or content when presenting apologetics to this generation?

Greg: I *love* this generation of young people. They are more open to engage in spiritual truth than any generation I can remember in my four decades on this planet. In my experience, postmoderns have been misdiagnosed as being purely relational—they are rational as well and hungry to explore spiritual truth. Therefore we must equip Christian students to engage others effectively in spiritual conversations. Never with the end of winning the intellectual debate, but always with the end of awakening others to their need to deal with the question, who is Jesus?

Effective apologetics training motivates and equips students to help others in their search for spiritual truth and to point them toward the cross. At Dare 2 Share Ministries, we encourage youth leaders to use an A.L.T.-ernative teaching style with their students: Ask great questions. Listen intently. Teach God's truth. This circular learning process engages students in interaction, affirms the honesty of their comments, and challenges them to consider the biblical perspective. Then in turn, as students have opportunities to use their apologetics training in their spiritual conversations with others, they will have been mentored in how to ask great questions, listen intently, and teach God's truth.

Sean: What advice would you give for incorporating apologetics training into the life of the church today?

Greg: Apologetics training must be viewed as only one piece of the larger picture of evangelism. Christians must be trained and equipped to share the gospel like a love letter. We must not start out arguing. We must start by sharing the story of the gospel persuasively and powerfully. Apologetics should be tacked on like a P.S. at the end of the love letter. At the right time, we must be prepared to say, "Here's why I believe this to be true..." and then present a reasoned and compelling defense of the gospel.

Why? Because apologetics have never saved anyone. The gospel does that. Well-thought-out arguments support at best. But they do not save. They are important. But they are not as important as the gospel message. Therefore it is critical that Christians be trained to first share the gospel message clearly and then be prepared to follow up that message with reasoned apologetics.

> **Greg Stier** is the founder and president of Dare 2 Share and the author of several books, including *Venti Jesus Please, Ministry Mutiny, Dare 2 Share: A Field Guide for Sharing Your Faith,* and *Outbreak.*

STORYTELLING AND PERSUASION

by Brian Godawa

love apologetics. I've studied issues of defending the faith for more than 20 years. In fact, my Christianity has been shaped within an apologetic context. I've learned a lot of biblical doctrine by seeing how it contradicts various cults and worldviews. I've come to understand the nature of the "faith once for all delivered to the saints" in terms of rational defense of its propositions. I've defined my doctrinal beliefs through systematic theological objections to false doctrines. One might even say I've been obsessed with apologetics and rational inquiry.

I found in the Bible a justification for my love affair with reason. Paul persuaded people to repent (Acts 18:4), and the Greek word for "repent" means "to change the mind." God's revelation appeals to logical laws like those of identity (Exodus 3:14), antithesis (Exodus 20:3), and noncontradiction (Exodus 20:16), so often it's not even debatable. Oh, and by the way, Jesus used logic too (Matthew 21:24-27).

In my pursuit of rational discourse I came to love propositions.[1] They seemed to be so clarifying, so neat and tidy, in my quest to discover truth and reality. Scripture makes propositional truth claims. God is eternal, immortal, and invisible (1 Timothy 1:17). God is love (1 John 4:8). God knows all things (1 John 3:20) and works all things after the counsel of His will (Ephesians 1:11). These are just a few of the hundreds of propositional truths about God in the Bible.

I have become proficient using one of the most common approaches to defending the faith with unbelievers:

1. Prove the existence of God using the teleological, ontological, or other arguments for God's existence.

2. Prove the Bible is reliable history.

3. Prove the resurrection of Jesus Christ from the Bible.

I thought that being rigorously logical, empirically probable, and calmly rational was the most biblical means of persuading unbelievers. Of course, the Holy Spirit is the one who convicts and saves people, but my task was to provide for them the rational and empirical foundation upon which to rest their faith in a set of doctrinal propositions and historical facts.

Gradually, through an inordinate emphasis in my faith on logic and empirical and rational proofs, I had transformed my Christian faith into the scientific method. Rather than allowing my fear of the Lord to be the beginning of knowledge (Proverbs 1:7), human knowledge acquired through empirical observation and rational inquiry was the beginning of my faith. I had become a Christian Mr. Spock, preferring syllogism over story, proposition over metaphor, science over symbol, logic over emotion. All those messy metaphors, all that ambiguous figurative language, imprecise terminology, and unscientific poetic hyperbole in the Bible got in my way of clear and distinct ideas. Emotions seemed irrational and irrelevant because as all good logicians know, the appeal to pity (emotion) is an informal logical fallacy, and emotions cannot be trusted. Never mind that Jesus appealed to pity to persuade people (Luke 10:29-37). Never mind that God constantly uses an appeal to pity throughout the Scriptures (Jonah 4:10-11).[2] The appeal to emotion may be logically invalid, but it is biblically valid, and that haunted my intellect for years.

I came to realize that what I was lacking in my understanding of the faith and defense of it was story and imagination. I surveyed the Bible and found that about 30 percent of it is propositional truth, and about 70 percent of it is story and imagination (that is, narrative, metaphor, symbol, image, and poetry).[3] Yes, Scripture contains propositional and doctrinal truth, but these are communicated through story, not systematic theology or scientific discourse. Yes, the Bible includes rationality and empirical facts, but these are embedded within a more primary emphasis on storytelling. The Bible is essentially one big story about how God will redeem His people through election, exodus, exile, and eschatological return under Messiah. Jesus didn't come to teach us abstract doctrines of individualistic salvation like a wandering sage. He came to embody the climax of God's story of redemption of His people.[4]

I looked closer at Jesus' ministry. Did He teach dogmatics from a pulpit? No. Jesus taught about the kingdom of God mostly through parables—sensate, dramatic stories. To Him, the kingdom was far too deep and rich a truth to entrust to rational abstract propositions. He chose stories of weddings, investment bankers, unscrupulous slaves, and buried treasure instead of syllogisms, abstraction, systematic, or dissertations. Jesus could do abstraction. He preferred not to. And He remained an enigma to the unbeliever. He did not explain His imaginative stories and metaphors to those who did not have ears to hear.

Indeed, stories and parables may be superior means of conveying theological truth than propositional logic or theological abstraction. As N.T. Wright suggests, "it would be clearly quite wrong to see these stories as mere illustrations of truths that could in principle have been articulated in a purer, more abstract form."[5] He reminds us that theological terms like "monotheism" "are late constructs, convenient shorthands for sentences with verbs in them [narrative], and... sentences with verbs in them are the real stuff of theology, not mere childish expressions of a 'purer' abstract truth."[6]

I discovered Kenneth E. Bailey, an expert on Middle Eastern culture, who explains that "a biblical story is not simply a 'delivery system' for an idea. Rather, the story first creates a world and then invites the listener to live in that world, to take it on as part of who he or she is...In reading and studying the Bible, ancient tales are not examined merely in order to extract a theological principle or ethical model."[7] Theologian Kevin Vanhoozer agrees that doctrinal propositions are not "more basic" than the narrative, and in fact, they fail to communicate what narrative can. He writes in his book *The Drama of Doctrine,* "Narratives make story-shaped points that cannot always be paraphrased in propositional statements without losing something in translation."[8] Claiming that the "ultimate meaning" of the parable of the Good Samaritan is simply that we should love or help the marginalized does not contain the full truth that comes only with telling the story with all its characters and emotions. If you try to scientifically dissect a parable, you will kill it, and if you discard the carcass once you have your doctrine, you have discarded the heart of God.

Because of my modern Western bias toward rational theological discourse, I was easily blinded to the biblical emphasis on dramatic storytelling. I considered stories to be quaint illustrations of abstract doctrinal universal truths. But God uses stories as His dominant means of incarnating truth. And as I began to look at the Bible with this different paradigm, I saw what I did not see before with my modernist mind-set. Even New Testament apologetics is story driven.

If It's Good Enough for the Apostle Paul...

In Acts 17:16-34, the apostle Paul engages in the only detailed example of New Testament apologetics in a pagan context. So it stands to reason (pun intended) that this should be a strong model for Christians who would defend the faith. In fact, this passage has been claimed by every school of apologetics, from evidentialism to presuppositionalism, in an attempt to justify its approach. One thing most of these differing viewpoints have in common is their emphasis on Paul's discourse as rational debate or empirical proof. What they all seem to miss is the narrative structure of his presentation. An examination of that structure reveals that Paul does not engage in dialectic so much as he does in storytelling. In essence, Paul retells the pagan Stoic story within a Christian framework, and in so doing, he subverts the Stoic story and captures it for the lordship of Christ.

Paul is speaking to poets and philosophers at the Areopagus in Athens. This setting was famous for drawing cultural leaders of the day to debate their philosophy through oration, poetry, and plays. The modern-day equivalent of Athens could arguably be Los Angeles or New York as the centers of media communications in the world. The Areopagus was also the name of the judicial body that formally examined and charged violators of the Roman law against illicit new religions.[9] Narratively, Luke casts Paul as a reflection of Socrates, someone with whom the Athenians would be both familiar and uncomfortable. It was Socrates who Xenophon said was condemned and executed for being "guilty of rejecting the gods acknowledged by the state and of bringing in new divinities."[10] Socrates' death was a shame upon Athens' history. Luke suggests that memory of shame by using a similar phrase to describe Paul when he conveys the accusation from some of the philosophers against Paul in verse 18: "He seems to be a proclaimer of strange deities." This technique of narrative analogy (Paul as a Socrates) is one of the ways in which storytelling persuades. Rationalists would consider that rhetorical tactic manipulative, but the Holy Spirit–inspired author Luke obviously did not.

Most apologists are aware that Paul explicitly quotes some Stoic poets in this passage (verse 28), but what many of them miss is that Paul is not merely quoting a couple authors in order to be relevant to his audience. He is following, in his own presentation, the implicit structure of Stoic storytelling about the universe itself. A comparison of Paul's oration with the Stoic Cleanthe's "Hymn to Zeus" will yield an almost point-by-point reflection.[11] In the interest of space and time, I will simply chart Paul's statements along with narrative elements of other Stoic or Greek philosophers that Paul is also reflecting.

> **Paul:** "Men of Athens, I observe that you are very religious in all respects."
> **Sophocles:** "Athens is held of states, the most devout."
> **Pausanias:** "Athenians more than others venerate the gods."[12]

Paul: "The God who made the world and all things in it, since He is Lord of heaven and earth, does not dwell in temples made with hands."

Zeno: "Temples are not to be built to the gods."[13]

Euripides: "What house fashioned by builders could contain the divine form within enclosed walls?"[14]

Paul: "Nor is He served by human hands, as though He needed anything, since He Himself gives to all people life and breath and all things."

Seneca: "God seeks no servants; He himself serves mankind."

Euripides: "God has need of nothing."[15]

Paul: "And He made from one man every nation of mankind."

Seneca: "Nature produced us related to one another, since she created us from the same source and to the same end."[16] "All persons, if they are traced back to their origins, are descendents of the gods."[17]

Dio Chrysostom: "It is from the gods that the race of men is sprung."[18]

Paul: "...to live on all the face of the earth, having determined their appointed times and the boundaries of their habitation."

Epictetus: "How else could things happen so regularly, by God's command as it were? When he tells plants to bloom, they bloom, when he tells them to bear fruit, they bear it...Is God [Zeus] then, not capable of overseeing everything and being present with everything and maintaining a certain distribution with everything?"[19]

Paul: "...that they would seek God, if perhaps they might grope for Him and find Him, though He is not far from each one of us."

Dio Chrysostom: "Primeval men are described as 'not settled separately by themselves far away from the divine being or outside him, but…sharing his nature.'"[20]

Seneca: "God is near you, He is with you, He is within you."[21]

Paul: "For in Him we live and move and exist, as even some of your own poets have said, 'For we also are His offspring.'"

Epimenides: They fashioned a tomb for thee, 'O holy and high one' / But thou art not dead; 'thou livest and abidest for ever,' / For in thee we live and move and have our being.[22]

Aratus: All the ways are full of Zeus, / And all the market-places of human beings. The sea is full / Of him; so are the harbors. In every way we have all to do with Zeus, / For we are truly his offspring.[23]

Paul: "We ought not to think that the Divine Nature is like gold or silver or stone, an image formed by the art and thought of man."

Epictetus: "You are a 'fragment of God'; you have within you a part of Him…Do you suppose that I am speaking of some external God, made of silver or gold? It is within yourself that you bear Him."[24]

Zeno: "Men shall neither build temples nor make idols."

Paul: "Therefore what you worship in ignorance, this I proclaim to you…Therefore having overlooked the times of ignorance…"

Dio Chrysostom: "How, then, could they have remained ignorant and conceived no inkling…[that] they were filled with the divine nature?"[25]

Epictetus: "You are a 'fragment of God'; you have within you a part of Him. Why then are you ignorant of your own kinship?"[26]

A few important observations are in order regarding Paul's reference to pagan poetry and non-Christian mythology. First, it points out that, as an orthodox Pharisee who stressed the separation of holiness, he did not consider it unholy to expose himself to the godless media and art forms (books, plays, and poetry) of his day. He did not merely familiarize himself with them, he *studied* them—well enough to be able to quote them and even utilize their narrative. Paul primarily quoted Scripture in his writings to believers, but to unbelievers here, he quotes from and uses unbelievers' writings.

Second, this appropriation of pagan cultural images and thought forms by biblical writers reflects more than a mere quoting of popular sayings or shallow cultural reference. It illustrates a redemptive interaction with those thought forms, a certain amount of involvement in and affirmation of the prevailing culture in service to the gospel. Paul's preaching in Acts 17 is not a shallow usage of mere phrases, but a deep structural identification with Stoic narrative and images that align with the gospel. He is not engaging in logical dialectic, but is telling a story within a subversive Christian framework of convergences with Stoicism. The list of convergences can be summarized like this:

Stoic Narrative	Verses in Acts 17
The incorporeal nature of God	24-25
God's self-sufficiency	25
The "oneness" or brotherhood of mankind	26
Providence over seasons and habitations	26
Humanity's blind groping	27
Pantheism and immanence	27-28
Zeus and Logos	28
Humans as God's offspring	28
Divine nature is not gold or silver	29
Wisdom versus ignorance	23,30
Justice	30-31

It is instructive to notice what Paul does *not* do as much as it is to notice what he does do. Paul uses language that Stoics and other Athenian pagans would recognize, yet he does not qualify it with distinction from the Christian worldview until the very end of the story. When Paul quotes the pagan poetry, he does not differentiate Yahweh from the Zeus of the poems. When he speaks of God's immanence, he does not deny the pantheism that Stoics would surely be assuming. He doesn't distinguish his "oneness in Adam" from the pantheist "oneness in the gods." He doesn't delineate biblical willing ignorance from the Stoic metaphysical ignorance. Paul may communicate Scriptural truth, but here, he never quotes the Bible as a source. He quotes pagan sources, much to the chagrin of modern fundamentalists. And when he does reference Jesus, he never uses Jesus' name, something he would no doubt be condemned for by modern evangelists. So, just what is Paul up to?

> **Paul:** "God is now declaring to men that all people everywhere should repent, because He has fixed a day in which He will judge the world in righteousness through a Man whom He has appointed, having furnished proof to all men by raising Him from the dead."

Here is where the subversion of Paul's storytelling rears its head. Everything is not as it seems. Paul the storyteller gets his pagan audience to nod their heads in agreement, only to be thrown for a loop at the end. Repentance, judgment, and the resurrection, all antithetical to Stoic beliefs, form the conclusion of Paul's narrative.

Ben Witherington concludes this about Paul's Areopagus speech:

> What has happened is that Greek notions have been taken up and given new meaning by placing them in a Jewish-Christian monotheistic context. Apologetics by means of defense and attack is being done, using Greek thought to make monotheistic points. The call for repentance at the end shows where the argument has been going all along—it is

not an exercise in diplomacy or compromise but ultimately a call for conversion.[27]

The Stoics believed in a "great conflagration" of fire, where the universe would end in the same kind of fire out of which it was created.[28] This was not the fire of damnation, however, as in Christian doctrine. It was rather the cyclical recurrence of what scientific theorists today would call the "oscillating universe." Everything would collapse into fire and then be recreated again out of that fire and relive the same cycle and development of history over and over again. Paul's call of final, linear, once-for-all judgment by a single man was certainly one of the factors, then, that caused some of these interested philosophers to scorn him.

The other factor sure to provoke the ire of the cosmopolitan Athenian culture shapers was the proclamation of the resurrection of Jesus. The poet and dramatist Aeschylus wrote what became a prominent Stoic slogan: "When the dust has soaked up a man's blood, once he is dead there is no resurrection."[29] Paul's explicit reference to the resurrection was certainly a part of the twist he used in his subversive storytelling to get the Athenians to listen to what they otherwise might ignore.

Subversion Versus Syncretism

Some Christians may react with fear that this kind of redemptive interaction with culture is syncretism, an attempt to fuse two incompatible systems of thought. Subversion, however, is not syncretism. Subversion is what Paul engaged in.

In subversion, the narrative, images, and symbols of one system are discreetly redefined or altered in the new system. Paul quotes a poem to Zeus but covertly intends a different deity. He superficially affirms the immanence of the Stoic Universal Reason that controls and determines all nature and men, yet he describes this universal all-powerful deity as personal rather than as abstract law. He agrees with the Stoics that men are ignorant of God and His justice, but then he affirms that God proved that He will judge the world through Christ by raising Christ from the dead—two doctrines the Stoics were vehemently against. He affirms the unity of humanity and the immanence of God in all things, but he contradicts Stoic pantheism and redefines that immanence by affirming God's transcendence and the Creator-creature distinction. And most revealing of all, Paul did not expose these stark differences between the gospel and the Stoic narrative until the end of his talk. He was subverting paganism, not syncretizing Christianity with it.

Subversive Story Strategy

By casting his presentation of the gospel in terms that Stoics could identify with and by undermining their narrative with alterations, Paul is strategically subverting through story. Author Curtis Chang, in his book *Engaging Unbelief,* explains this rhetorical strategy as three-fold:

1. entering the challenger's story
2. retelling the story
3. capturing that retold tale with the gospel metanarrative.[30]

He explains that the claim that we observe evidence objectively and apply reason neutrally to prove our worldview is an artifact of Enlightenment mythology. The truth is that each epoch of thought in history, whether Medieval, Enlightenment, or postmodern, is a contest in storytelling. "The one who can tell the best story, in a very real sense, wins the epoch."[31]

Chang affirms the inescapability of story and image through history even in philosophical argumentation: "Strikingly, many of the classic philosophical arguments from different traditions seem to take the form of a story: from Plato's scene of the man bound to the chair in the cave to Hobbes's elaborate drama of the 'state of nature,' to John Rawls's 'choosing game.' "[32] Stories may come in many different genres, but we cannot escape them any more than we can escape the use of reason.

The progression of events from creation to fall to redemption that characterizes Paul's narrative reflects the beginning, middle, and end of linear Western storytelling. God is Lord, He created all things and created all people from one (creation), and He determined the seasons and boundaries. People then became blind and were found groping in the darkness after Eden, ignorant of their very identity as His children (fall). Then God raised a man from the dead and will judge the world in the future through that same man. Through repentance, people can escape their ignorance and separation from God (redemption). Creation, fall, redemption; beginning, middle, end; Genesis, Covenant, Eschaton. These are elements of narrative that communicate worldview. And worldviews are ultimately *stories.*

Does this retelling of stories simply reduce persuasion to a relativistic standoff between opposing stories with no criteria for discerning which is true? Scholar N.T. Wright suggests that the way to handle the clash of competing stories is to tell yet another story, one that encompasses and explains the stories of one's opposition, yet contains an explanation for the anomalies or contradictions within those stories:

> There is no such thing as "neutral" or "objective" proof; only the claim that the story we are now telling about the world as a whole makes more sense, in its outline and detail, than other potential or actual stories that may be on offer. Simplicity of outline, elegance in handling the details within it, the inclusion of all the parts of the story, and the ability of the story to make sense beyond its immediate subject-matter: these are what count.[33]

Paul tells the story of mankind in Acts 17, a story that encompasses and includes images and elements of the Stoic story but solves the problems of that system within a more coherent and meaningful story that conveys Christianity. He studies and engages in the Stoic story, retells that story, and captures it with the gospel metanarrative. Paul subverts Stoic paganism through storytelling with the Christian worldview.

Another Example of Subversion

Earlier, I referred to Los Angeles and New York as a strong analogy to the influence of the Greek poets. I would like to conclude with an example of a Hollywood movie that uses subversive storytelling in a way similar to Paul on the Areopagus. *To End All Wars,* a movie that I wrote, was based on the true story of Ernest Gordon, an Allied prisoner of war under the Imperial Japanese in World War II. The story is about how Ernest and the other prisoners dealt with their suffering from atrocities inflicted on them by their captors. When Ernest arrives in the camp, he seeks to survive by protecting himself. As he experiences the sacrifice of a fellow Christian in the camp, he learns how to love his neighbor as himself. And by the end of the story, he and his campmates are faced with the dilemma of what it means to love their enemy when the tables are turned.

The film explores the Eastern, Japanese mind-set as a collectivist culture that denigrates the value of the individual, which results in grave punishment for disobedience to hierarchy. The Western mind-set, as illustrated in the Allies, is a Darwinian individualist culture that elevates the individual at the expense of the community. Survival of the fittest is its ethic. But rather than a typical East-meets-West story, where one of the views is considered superior, *To End All Wars* illustrates that both East (collectivism) and West (individualism) are wrong extremes. A higher kingdom unites the one and the many, the community and the individual, with a proper unity and balance. That kingdom is the kingdom of God.

The kingdom of God subverts both the Eastern and Western worldviews by drawing upon the value that each contains in the group (East) and the individual (West). So Ernest and the Allies learn the value of the community and sacrifice of the individual, and the Imperial Japanese, with their understanding of self-sacrifice, are shown to have access to the gospel in a way that even the Westerners do not. And forgiveness is achievable for all.

A Los Angeles faith-based initiative, Cloud and Fire Ministries, has been showing *To End All Wars* to incarcerated at-risk youth in detention centers in Southern California. The initiative is federally funded, so workers are not allowed to proselytize for their faith. But they are allowed to show the movie, which communicates the gospel and forgiveness through story to the kids in a way they will listen to. They would never pay attention to the same gospel message from some middle-class Christian preacher or suburban white boy. As they identify the Bushido warrior code of the movie with their own gang codes on the street, they are drawn into the story that transcends all our differences and subverts the system, drawing their souls toward forgiveness. Storytelling can persuade and unify where rational debate and cultural differences only divide.

The conventional image of a Christian apologist is one who studies apologetics or philosophy at a university, one who wields logical arguments for the existence of God and manuscript evidence for the reliability of the Bible, or one who engages in intellectual debates about comparative religions or current scientific skepticism. These remain valid and important endeavors, but in a postmodern world focused on narrative discourse, we need also to take a lesson from the apostle Paul and expand our avenues for evangelism and defending the faith. We need more Christian apologists writing revisionist stories based on godless deities such as Darwin, Marx, and Freud; writing for and subverting pagan TV sitcoms; bringing a Christian worldview interpretation to their journalism in secular magazines and news reporting; making horror films that undermine the idol of post-Enlightenment modernity as did *The Exorcism of Emily Rose;* and writing, singing, and playing subversive industrial music, rock music, and rap music. We need to be actively, sacredly subverting the secular stories of the culture and restoring their fragmented narratives for Christ.

Storytelling is not just a second-class citizen in apologetics that is merely acceptable but subordinate to rational dialectic and empirical observation. Storytelling is the dominant means that the Bible uses to communicate and persuade because storytelling is at the heart of human identity created in the image of a storytelling God.

Brian Godawa is the screenwriter for the award-winning feature film *To End All Wars* and author of *Hollywood Worldviews: Watching Films with Wisdom and Discernment*. This article was adapted from his forthcoming book *Word Pictures: Knowing God Through Story and Imagination*.

APOLOGETICS AND EMOTIONAL DEVELOPMENT: UNDERSTANDING OUR WAYS OF KNOWING AND FINDING MEANING

by Mark Matlock

n 2001, David Kinnaman, president and strategic leader of the Barna Group, helped me put a survey project together examining the beliefs and behaviors of American teenagers. One of the most significant trends we observed was that students with a set of seven basic doctrinal beliefs stood apart from the rest of the crowd of self-professed Christian teens, teens who regularly attended church, and students who passed a simple two-question litmus test regarding why they considered themselves Christian.[1]

Later, we conducted another survey examining the supernatural beliefs of students and found similar results.[2] Students who held to a core of seven basic doctrinal beliefs differed profoundly from their peers when it came to beliefs in the supernatural and experimenting with occult activities.

Correlation does not always imply causation, but I couldn't help but believe that students with a solid understanding of core doctrines shared a healthy worldview that empowered them to live better. My practical conclusion: Teach doctrine. Why not?

But as I set out to teach basic doctrines to students in small groups, in one-on-one situations, and in larger group settings, I began to notice something intriguing. Some students readily absorbed truth presented rationally, but for others, it didn't seem to penetrate into their being. This made me curious. What factors may be present in the lives of those who readily absorb and those who repel rationalistic explanations of biblical truth?

I began several less scientific, more casual experiments with students and found that it had little to do with whether they were introverted or extroverted, abstract thinkers or concrete. In fact, it didn't even seem to matter if they were initially open or hostile to Christianity. Rather, those who were able to absorb propositional statements of doctrinal truths best were those who were emotionally healthy.

I shared these findings with a doctor friend, and he dropped Daniel Goleman's book *Emotional Intelligence: Why It Can Matter More than IQ* on my doorstep and said I might find some interesting leads between the covers. Needless to say, I did. Goleman's work triggered a series of inquiries into ground-breaking research in neurobiology. These helped me understand more about Jesus' messages, the way He conveyed truth, and how we can communicate truth and love in community.

Hardwired to Connect

In 2003 the YMCA, Dartmouth Medical School, and the Institute for American Values hosted a symposium of specialists to ask why violence and depression were noticeably increasing among children and adolescents.

Their report, "Hardwired to Connect," looked at a broad overview of research in various fields, including new understanding coming from the expanding field of neurobiology.[3] What they concluded was nothing short of amazing, and I'm still shocked by how few youth pastors and pastors have heard of the study or its findings.

The principle finding of this study was that science is increasingly demonstrating that the human person is hardwired to connect. We need close attachments to other people, beginning with mothers and fathers and family and then to the larger community we live in. Also, we are hardwired for meaning, born with a built-in capacity and drive to search for purpose and to reflect on life's ultimate ends. If these two needs are not met, children cannot be expected to be healthy and develop.

This is quite a statement from a group representing diverse fields of academia! What is more, the study shows that primary nurturing relationships influence early spiritual development, that spirituality significantly influences well-being, and that the human brain appears to be organized to ask ultimate questions and seek ultimate answers.

Because you are reading this book on apologetics, I'm sure these conclusions are hardly surprising to you. We know most people are searching for truth in some fashion because we engage people in this conversation every day. The need is so real that people will believe the most ridiculous things (remember the Hale-Bopp comet?) to have these needs satisfied. Now we have scientific evidence for a biological need to address these issues, and that is significant for several reasons.

Some emotionally unhealthy people cling to apologetics and abuse it relationally.

At the time of this writing, a preponderance of books addresses the subject of human irrationality as it relates to decision making. Few people make decisions based on sound arguments as opposed to gut feelings. Emotions can be tricky, but that doesn't mean we should ignore them as we employ apologetics.

As a teenager who was fascinated with apologetics, I sometimes used my arguments to announce the judgment of God and not to lovingly invite people come to follow Christ. I spoke truth, but I had convinced myself the goal was to win others over to my way of thinking, not to restore their relationship to a holy God.

So we need to be aware of the possibility of apologetical abuse in our own lives, but we should guard against it in those we disciple as well. This abuse and the relative emotional unhealthiness of many apologetically bent believers have caused others to dismiss good thinking and solid evidence for our faith as unnecessary. Nothing could be further from the truth!

People need some emotional health to accept God's truth.

Think of a time when you had a spiritual breakthrough, an experience that you might label as a spiritual transformation. It may have been your salvation or a subsequent step of growth. Reflect on that event. What brought it on? It was most likely a result of a relationship with another person.

When a church I formerly attended suffered a split, I was challenged in many positive ways to mature in my faith. The experience of mentors in my life has also led to great moments of change. For whatever reason, God uses healthy relationships in our lives to help us grow. But what if those relationships do not exist or are unhealthy?

A big conclusion in the "Hardwired to Connect" report is the restoration of what the authors call "authoritative community." Morality, values, and faith are passed on through relationships, and the breakdown of community has caused emotional blocks that keep people from receiving truth. In the next section I'll explore how unhealthy relationships act as filters that keep us from experiencing God's truth.

Some aspects of current postmodernism may be symptoms of epidemic relational fracture in our society.

Relativism is clearly a very real phenomenon among our culture. This shift in philosophy and epistemology could be the result of the breakdown in community, not a rejection of the concept of truth. If my conjecture has any merit, we will not solve the problem of relativism with sharp arguments only, but with well-constructed arguments *and* healthy communities that care for one another. The letters to the early church are chock-full of direction for developing proper doctrine *and* for building healthy community (particularly James' epistle). Could it be that the healing experienced by members of early church was the result of biblical community as well as sound doctrine?

Recognizing the Holism in Our Ways of Knowing

The research supporting "Hardwired to Connect" got me thinking about how we connect to meaning in truth in a much more holistic manner than merely through the logical mind. The report speaks of "attachments," and that led me to an inquiry into attachment theory.

In the early 1900s, infants placed in foundling institutions died in extremely high numbers. John Bowlby observed that the infants in these facilities were managed very efficiently with various caretakers rolling through their shifts to make sure the children were fed and changed appropriately. But the caretakers were not assigned to particular children. They were assigned simply to the caretaking tasks, regardless of the children involved. Bowlby hypothesized that the children were dying because they were not bonding with caretakers in the way a child would with a parent.

By helping caretakers to establish more individualized relationships with children, foundling homes were able to drastically lower the mortality rate of infants. Indeed, we have a biological need for relationships! We die without them. Since Bowlby's time, psychologists, sociologists, and neurophysicians have built on his initial work and are learning how the biology of relationships works.

Some of the most significant findings have led to attachment theory. The basis of this theory is that we all need to make secure attachments with others. That begins with our first caretakers—usually our parents—and then includes relationships in the larger community around us. If we can't make secure attachments, we make insecure ones, and that can negatively impact our emotional health.

These secure and insecure attachments shape the way the brain interprets life and creates meaning. This shaping occurs before the age of two, when our autobiographical memory kicks in—before we are even biologically capable of remembering anything about ourselves! Even though these patterns are formed early in the mind, they can be altered over time, but this is not easy to do.

Dr. Todd Hall at Rosemead School of Psychology has done some interesting work applying attachment theory to our relationship with God.[4] If insecure human attachments keep us from healthy connections with others, couldn't they keep us from connecting with God as well? Dr. Hall's research has helped us understand that yes, if we are not securely attached to humans, we will struggle to have a secure attachment to God.

Instantly this made sense to me. Some of my students were incredibly intelligent and even showed an interest in Christ, but they never seemed to make the breakthrough. I was trying to convince them of the evidence for Christ, and they just couldn't get it. Looking back, I realize many of those students were emotionally wounded (or even abandoned) individuals who simply could not connect to what I was saying. I now wonder if a biological barrier kept them from understanding the truth. I wasn't able to see the barrier at the time, and maybe I was too emotionally immature to offer them the love and acceptance they needed.

Two Ways of Knowing

In the debates between John F. Kennedy and Richard Nixon, an interesting phenomenon occurred. Those who heard the debates tended to feel Nixon made the stronger appeal. But on television, Kennedy was favored. Nixon had been ill that night and didn't look good. On the radio, this information wasn't available, so only the words of the candidates influenced listeners.

These debates and a host of other media examples continue to reinforce what neurobiologists now understand biologically. We actively call on two systems of knowing to create meaning in our world. Dr. Dan Siegel in *The Developing Mind* offers this simple framework of explicit and implicit knowing.

Explicit knowing is what we are most familiar with. This knowing involves our verbal language, is logical and linear, searches for causes and effects, uses words to describe the world, and is typically what we use in our right-and-wrong thinking. Explicit knowledge is what is often referred to as left-brain thinking.

Implicit knowing, on the other hand (or side of the brain), happens without much conscious thought, and it often influences our thinking most. Implicit knowledge contrasts with explicit knowledge because it is nonlinear, holistic, and nonverbal.

Implicit knowledge drives our relationships because it processes automatically and is not under our direct control. Explicit knowledge is important, but we must integrate it with implicit knowledge if we are to love God and others fully.

In apologetics we typically deal in the realm of explicit knowledge when we make an argument. But what is happening on the implicit level is also important if we want our message to be heard. People assess how much we sincerely care about them when we present a message, and they are quickly able to determine whether the message we offer seems to be true in our own lives. We cannot simply have good arguments; our lives must reflect the presence of the Holy Spirit's life in us.

Recently I watched two young men reenact a skit they saw my friends The Skit Guys perform. It was horrible! These two students had used exactly the same script as the seasoned performers used, yet nobody laughed. Why?

They possessed the explicit information (the script) but had not yet mastered the implicit information of character, timing, body movement, and interpersonal chemistry that the others had already acquired. In fact, The Skit Guys do some material that works only because the majority of people at an event already have a relationship with them. Take out the relational history, and the material wouldn't work. A lot more is happening than the script alone can contain.

Sometimes I feel that this has hurt us when we use apologetics to witness. We borrow the script from our favorite authors, but we don't have the lifestyle and relationship to back it up when we recite it. The arguments are solid, but the message never makes it past the messenger. As we train young people to use apologetic arguments, we must also be sure they are ready to engage others with the same love and respect Jesus displayed.

Two Ways of Remembering

Just as there are two ways of knowing, Dr. Siegel also described two types of memory that fit into the explicit and implicit systems.

Sometimes we explicitly know we are remembering something, but sometimes we remember things without conscious awareness. Phobias are often associated with memories we have consciously forgotten long ago. But when something triggers that memory implicitly, we can experience deep and powerful feelings without understanding why.

A student I worked with refused to go to church. She would attend a home Bible study, but she would never come to a service at church. Some friends finally convinced her to attend, and I watched her as the service progressed. She was tense and fighting back tears. Eventually she got up and left.

I knew something was going on in her, but I completely misread the signals and interpreted her actions to mean that she was hostile to God. After all, she was indeed a pretty rough person and had a hard time accepting the gospel in her life. Still, she kept hanging around and never completely rejected it.

In my immaturity, I never realized that her history involved some abuse by a deeply iconic religious member of her family. She wanted to believe God was good, but something in her implicit memory system triggered her feelings. She wasn't thinking about the abuse when she was having the reactions.

Can these implicit memories impact our understanding of truth? Dr. Hall thinks so, and he talks about attachments forming a filter that keeps us from connecting to God, to others, and to meaning.[5] Dr. Hall performed a series of studies comparing people's explicit behaviors (such as reading their Bibles, going to church, and spending time in prayer) to their implicit relational filters to determine their effect on spiritual health.[6] What he found was interesting: People with unhealthy connections to God were just as likely to engage in the same explicit Christian behaviors as those with healthy relationships to God. This means that we often measure the wrong actions when trying to determine true spiritual health.

As we pursue the study and application of apologetics in the new millennium, we must be even more mindful that this truth we speak of is about a relationship with God that results in a relationship with the body of Christ. We live in a broken and disconnected society, where relationships are shattered, so the explicit truth of our message is not enough in itself for many people. They will hear it only when we are also concerned about and aware of the emotional well-being of others. This means integrating the explicit and implicit knowledge systems so the message of Christ can be fully heard.

Mark Matlock is president of WisdomWorks Ministries, the founder of PlanetWisdom student conferences, and the author of numerous books for teens, including the Wisdom On series. He now serves with Youth Specialties.

AN INTERVIEW WITH JEFF MYERS

Sean McDowell: What topics in apologetics seem to be especially relevant and important to this generation?

Jeff Myers: My thoughts on this question come from the work I've done with students at Summit Ministries in the last few years. The number one question that comes up is, why does God allow bad things to happen? I've realized, along with the other speakers who do much of the personal counseling and mentoring, that what students are really asking is, why does God allow bad things to happen to *me*?

Pluralism is also a big question, but there has been a substantial shift in the way students approach it. In the past we could give talks on the cults and world religions while assuming that students were looking for ways to justify their Christian beliefs against the alternatives. Now they seem to have no desire to do that—they wonder why we're being so "mean" to people who "have the right to believe whatever they want."

Sean: Do we need to make substantial changes in our approach or content when presenting apologetics to this generation?

Jeff: I think we do need to make changes. Some people wonder whether the majority of kids in this generation is prepared to think through *any* issues in an in-depth fashion. I've been reading a book called *The Dumbest Generation*. The prophecies of Neil Postman and Jaeques Ellul about the dumbing-down effect of the mass media seem to have come true.

Still, these are relational students, so I think we need to prepare them for arguing contextually rather than linearly. They may not have many opportunities to present a logical case, but the big issues sometimes do come up in everyday conversations, and they'll need to know how to address them. This will include engaging others in respectful but rigorous conversation.

Sean: What advice would you give for incorporating apologetics training into the life of the church today?

Jeff: Pastors should clearly articulate that any question asked respectfully is a good question and deserves an answer. I don't know how to say this without sounding like a heretic, but here goes: We should stop trying to develop a watertight apologetic. I'm not giving up on the primacy of Scripture or my conviction that Scripture is absolutely true, but I have stopped attempting to communicate to students that I have everything locked down or that such-and-such an argument is so logically defensible that it will leave an opponent stumped. I've seen far too many students become arrogant because they thought they had the best arguments. Then they encountered sincere and intelligent people who believed the opposite. At first they were shocked, then intrigued, then open, and then persuaded by the other point of view. We must emphasize the importance of strong thinking skills as well as humility in making our arguments.

> **Jeff Myers** is president of Passing the Baton International and associate professor of communication studies at Bryan College.

MAKING APOLOGETICS COME ALIVE IN YOUTH MINISTRY

by Alex McFarland

In early 2001, news wire services reported that huge Buddhist statues in Afghanistan's Bahaim Valley were being destroyed by members of the Taliban. The area had long been the site of many monasteries, and their centuries-old statues were being blown apart as horrified monks looked on. One statue—thought to have been carved from a type of sandstone—turned out to be made of gold. Perhaps the golden statue was covered over with mud many years ago in order to hide it from looters. Uncovered by artillery and bombs, something assumed to be mere dirt was revealed to be a priceless treasure.

This story reminds me of the true value of apologetics and of the reaction some church leaders have to the subject. Though some leaders ignore Christian apologetics or have a fairly low opinion of it, I believe that apologetics can yield priceless dividends for the church. In the lives of teens especially, the teaching of apologetics is potentially golden.

Apologetics may be dismissed by some as being "old paradigm" or somehow counterproductive. As for youth ministry, apologetics is often assumed not to be relevant to the lives of teens or too complicated. I disagree. I think we set the intellectual bar way too low. Youth ministry should promote (among other things) critical thinking skills and the embrace of a biblical view in all areas of life. Many Christian teens are *never* intellectually stretched at church. For fear of losing teens' interest or for fear that we'll appear boring, youth ministry has fallen short of imparting the deep truths of Christianity.

Christian Teens and Their Skeptical Friends

Even if most Christian teens don't use the term "apologetics," they seek the results that good apologetics can provide. I think of Devin, a young lady who was part of a Christian club that was allowed to meet at her public school. Some unchurched students came, asking about the Discovery Channel program on the supposed tomb of Jesus. Another student, skeptical about Christianity, had brought from the school library the National Geographic magazine with the cover story about the Gospel of Judas. What would be the club members' response to such news items?

The teens—both Christian and non-Christian—easily connected the theological dots. Here was a high-profile documentary asserting that Jesus hadn't risen from the dead. If that were true, Christianity would fall. Here was an article that impugned the trustworthiness of the four canonical Gospels, preferring the eclectic content of Gnostic writings instead. If this journalist were correct, then almost 2000 years of trust in the New Testament would have to be reconsidered.

As Devin described the club situation to me, she said, "My friends are open to belief, but they all say, 'Show us the evidence!'" Devin spoke with passion, emphasizing her point by hitting the edge of the table. "My youth leader said you could help us get answers to share with our friends."

Devin didn't use the word "apologetics," but that is what her club's ministry opportunity required. Apologetics and doctrine should be a part of every church's youth ministry! In my experience, Christian teens want to know the reasons why we believe what we believe. It's funny—I've never had a teen say to me, "My generation cares more about relationships than about truth." Never. Or, "Feelings are what convinces me of a point; evidence doesn't matter at all." No student I've interacted with has said, "Alex, please stop! Don't you know that people our age aren't smart enough to understand Christianity?"

Timeless Truth with Daily Value

I am often asked if apologetics has real-life, personal application in youth ministry. Adult leaders sometimes question how relevant deep theological issues are to the average teen. "I'm not sure how many of my students are going around wondering about how to explain the Trinity," one youth pastor recently said to me.

But believers of every age group should be taught to think with precision about spiritual issues, apologetics content, and the components of a Christian worldview. For one thing, the Bible commands us to do this. But additionally, conveyance of such truths touches both those who are strong in their faith and those who may be struggling.

I was reminded of the value of apologetics recently while talking with Ken, an 18-year-old. He was convinced that his sinful past—a history of sexual promiscuity, drug use, and altercations with the law—meant that he had become guilty of the unpardonable sin. It became clear to me that part of his struggle was due to an incorrect view of God. I explained that if he was "unsavable" (as he called himself), that would mean that God was either unable or unwilling to forgive him.

Ken listened intently as we talked about characteristics which logically apply to God, including the fact that He is all-powerful and all-good. It was a beautiful thing to see Ken's facial expression brighten as he understood that God was both willing and able to forgive his sins. Later, Ken asked me to e-mail him a recap of our conversation and added, "I have some friends I want to talk with about how we can know that God is real."

Common Questions and "The Big Five"

Questions, questions, questions. Teens have an almost unlimited supply of them! A young man named Doug recently explained his struggles over the issue of whether he could trust the Bible: "An online skeptic site says that the Bible has to be fallible because it was written by fallible people." Doug asked, "How can you say that the Bible is supernatural when it was written by mortals?"

How about this one: "Truth means different things to different people. Couldn't something be true for one person but not for another?" Many teens have had their Christian perspective dismissed with statements such as these.

So which apologetics issues should you tackle in your youth ministry? Allow your teens to anonymously submit their "If You Could Ask God Anything" questions, and you'll get many a week's worth of thought-provoking lesson ideas! Here are just a few of the subjects I have fielded at teen events in recent weeks. Some are not really questions, but the observations beg a response:

> Could God cause Himself to go out of existence?

> How could God really hear the prayers of so many people?

> Sometimes God feels so far away.

> My father says that for centuries Christians have presented the ideas of Paul rather than the true teachings of Jesus, and that this is a mistake.

> If I become a Christian, will I have to give up things that I enjoy, and spend all my time bugging people about what they believe?

> Has archeology proven the Bible? If so, how?

> Don't homosexuals have the right not to be hated by the church?

> How does the Bible differ from the prophecies of Nostradamus?

> Who decided which books would be included in the Bible?

> How can I share Christ with this Muslim guy at my school?

> Is white magic bad? Some people I know are into it, but say that they are Christians too.

> Most teens I know wouldn't change their minds even if an apologist could refute their position. What I think would

be potent would be someone whose life is truly passionate for Jesus Christ.

As you can see, some questions deal with various spiritual issues, some are more about how to correctly respond to an external circumstance, and others reflect the need for basic information about the Christian worldview. For the busy youth leader, one of the perks of apologetics is that it provides endless ideas for content!

The volume of teaching options related to apologetics is almost limitless, but some basic apologetics issues represent the bare minimum of what students should be taught. Which core truths should your teens know before they leave youth group and head off for college and adult life? Here is my top-five list:

1. Truth: Does absolute, universal truth exist?

2. God: Can we know that He exists?

3. Scripture: How can we be sure that the Bible is trustworthy?

4. Jesus: Is He really the one and only Savior?

5. The problem of pain: Why does a supposedly loving God allow suffering in the world?

Knowledge of apologetics will enhance the effectiveness of your teens' walk and witness. For the saved and the seekers, Christianity has—and *is*—the answer.

Practical Suggestions for Apologetics with Youth

1. The vision to equip and evangelize through apologetics must be held by the ministry leadership. Endeavor to see apologetics presented, promoted, accepted, and taught within your church's youth ministry. Identify where apologetics content can be integrated into existing programs. The goal is to help teens become more committed followers of Christ and integrate their faith into all areas of thinking, learning, and doing.

2. Overcome resistance or fear of change. Don't tell yourself that some kids will be bored. If you don't do apologetics, some kids may be lost!

3. Communicate the need for apologetics. Staff, volunteers, and youth must understand why knowledge of apologetics is necessary.

4. Inform students of the biblical mandate for a defense of the faith. Share verses like 2 Corinthians 10:5; 2 Timothy 2:15; Titus 1:9; 1 Peter 3:15; and Jude 3. Remind your flock of Scriptures like Matthew 28:18-20 and Mark 16:15, in which God instructs believers to present the message of Jesus Christ to every age group of people.

5. Educate parents and youth on the benefits of apologetics. To a large degree, the benefits of apologetics are immediate and obvious. Share examples of well-known leaders who have been reached because of the evidence for Christianity. As you utilize apologetics-based content in the lives of teens, testimonies from your own group will become plentiful.

6. Present apologetics-oriented messages. Teach a lesson on apologetics in general or on a specific topic. Provide an apologetics-oriented teaching series. Here are some teaching ideas and styles that can be tailored to best meet the needs of your group:

- *Lecture.* This is effective when addressing large groups.

- *Lecture with discussion.* You may want to prepare one or two questions and individuals ahead of time to get the discussion rolling.

- *Video.* Visit www.theapologeticsbookstore.com for ideas. Watch Ben Stein's excellent film *Expelled: No Intelligence Allowed.* Rent Lee Strobel's video *The Case for Christ.* You can find plenty of options.

- *Panel of experts.* You may wish to host something like this on a quarterly basis. Invite three to five people to sit on a panel and tackle a topic.

- *Open forum.* This can be a very memorable and productive approach for outreach and teaching. Planning this will be contingent upon having access to one or more persons who can competently answer the questions. A neutral facilitator or moderator should control the mic and should gently prevent any one person in the audience from dominating the discussion.

- *Small group study and discussion.* This is a great format because the small size allows participation from everyone.

- *Case studies.* Biblically analyze a topic, individual, issue, or current event. Examples could include formulating a Christian response to Islam, researching how professed atheists like Bart Ehrman or John Loftis could leave their Christian faith, discussing and critiquing the resurgence of atheism, or providing a Christian response to a news items.

- *Role playing.* This can be a serious exercise with ample opportunity for learning. Have students research and argue a point with which they don't agree. Have another student respond, critiquing the other's position or defending the Christian view.

- *Reports.* Allow teens to study a topic and give a presentation at a certain date. These assignments worked especially well with a Sunday school class of middle schoolers my wife and I led for several years. Eventually, even the most reluctant participants were *asking* me to assign them an apologetics topic that they could share with the class! Allow room for the teens' creativity in the presentations. PowerPoint presentations or drama skits are welcome as long as they have solid apologetics content!

- *Worksheets and surveys.* These allow teens to communicate freely without being influenced by others.

- *Guest speakers.* Allocate a budget for bringing in local and national apologetics speakers. Several church youth groups could share the cost of one large event.

- *Apologetics conference.* Plan your own apologetics event, invite a well-known apologist to speak in your church, or consider hosting a regional event. Great options are available, such as Focus on the Family's Dig Deeper weekends or their Big Dig national events.

- *Debates.* This can be an effective means of engaging your community, provided certain parameters are observed. Invest much time in prayer before committing to a debate, and make sure the right parties are invited. The person representing Christianity should be a positive witness, consistently gracious, and of course, intellectually credible. Treat the debate opponent in a loving and Christlike manner at all times. I have hosted and participated in several apologetics debates with positive results. For a debate, my personal preference is that the selected venue be a school or local auditorium and not a church sanctuary.

7. Maximize on what's happening in the culture. Think about how many current events and social happenings touch on issues related to Christianity: the so-called "Blasphemy Challenge" on YouTube, the Chronicles of Narnia movies, "The Lost Tomb of Jesus," the Gospel of Thomas, Islam versus the world, gay marriage, abortion…the list seems endless.

8. Make apologetics practical. Explain how apologetics fosters intimacy with God. Hear testimonies from those whose faith was strengthened or who were able to share their faith more effectively.

9. Evaluate existing ministry programs. Consider how apologetics may be integrated into existing programs.

10. Identify teens and adults who have the ability and willingness to assist. Appoint an individual with leadership skills and apologetics interest who serves as your point person.

11. Send teen and adult leaders to apologetics training seminars. More options are available than ever before, including the National Conference on Christian Apologetics, the Big Dig, Frank Turek's CrossExamined weekends, and others.

12. The most important thing is to cover the teen apologetics ministry in prayer!

A Word About Resources

We are living in a golden age for apologetics resources! Recent decades of apologetics momentum has brought to the body of Christ many potent resources and several generations of first-rate scholars. Even at the risk of appearing self-serving, I offer some of my own resources because they were strategically developed through 20 years of apologetics ministry to teens:

Stand: Core Truths You Must Know for an Unshakable Faith (Tyndale). This book explains the basic doctrines of Christianity and provides reasons why believers have held to them for 2000 years. A free, downloadable small-group guide is available online from Tyndale.

Stand Strong in College (Tyndale). This book addresses the four areas in which a teen's faith will be tested in the time immediately following graduation. Teens throughout America were interviewed in the preparation for this book, and the spiritual journeys of six actual students are examined as they navigate the college years. An appendix presents practical answers for 20 apologetics issues that Christian students are sure to face on the university campus.

The Ten Most Common Objections to Christianity (Regal Books). Having spoken in nearly 1000 different locations—churches, schools, colleges, and even jails—I have been asked a lot of questions. Here are the ten I've heard most frequently, along with in-depth answers. In the back of the book is a 12-week small-group lesson guide.

These books cover the basics of apologetics, and all are written at a seventh-grade reading level. I also enthusiastically recommend the wonderful resources created by authors like Chuck Colson, Josh McDowell, Lee Strobel, Sean McDowell, Norman Geisler, and others. You may want to take a look at *Understanding the Times* by Summit Ministries' founder, David Noebel. I enthusiastically recommend the Truth Project series, produced by Focus on the Family and featuring top-notch communicator Del Tackett.

Apologetics Is for You!

According to the U.S. Census Bureau, in 2003, 73 million children in the United States were under 18 years old. Certainly, this number has increased by now. More teens are in America than ever, and more belief systems are competing for their hearts and minds!

I wrote this chapter with several potential readers in mind. First, this information is for everyone who wants each of these millions of teens to meet Christ and to grow spiritually. Apologetics is for every person who is passionate about instilling a Christian worldview in the lives of the next generation.

This material is also written to help you keep your outreach to teens interesting and inviting. Titus 2:10 (NIV) encourages Christian leaders in every way to "make the teaching about God our Savior attractive." We should strive to connect with our listeners and communicate with authenticity and relevancy. Also, more than ever, we need discernment and cultural sensitivity so we don't unintentionally repel someone we were hoping to draw.

But we must remember that our calling is to faithfully present Christ and the full panorama of biblical truth. Christians don't have to shy away from any questions or topics for lack of evidence supporting the faith. The lines of evidence affirming Christianity are plentiful, and they are persuasive. That's great! But neither should we be reluctant to present audiences with the deep realities of the faith for fear we'll lose them. Youth leader, I challenge you: Go deep. Let's see the dumbing down of our faith ended in this generation! Your teens will thank you for it, and they'll be stimulated, acquire more thirst for spiritual knowledge, and grow!

It is a precious thing to watch God's truth prompt within teens the desire for more and more depth. I have seen God use apologetics to ignite something special in the hearts and lives of countless teens throughout this nation. And nothing about the content had to be truncated in achieving this. I speak to middle and high schoolers with the same language I use when speaking to graduate students. And teens thank me for treating them as an intellectual peer.

Regarding apologetics and the faith challenges of our era, the key for adult leaders today is to be proactive rather than reactive. Don't wait until one of your former student leaders returns for a visit after graduation and announces that he or she has bailed out spiritually. The time to incorporate apologetics and worldview content into your student ministry is now—*today!*

Alex McFarland is the president of Southern Evangelical Seminary and the Veritas Graduate School. He also serves Focus on the Family as a speaker and writer for teen apologetics.

HOME-FIELD ADVANTAGE

by Chris Sherrod

Please help! My son isn't living out what he believes!" After hearing this desperate plea from parents far too many times, the heartbreaking truth that I've often had to explain is that their children actually *are* living out what they believe. Some can fake it for a while, but when kids just *appear* to be Christians, it's just a matter of time before their true beliefs surface. The life they've been living has either been the best way to avoid conflict or merely their faith tradition. As they are confronted with life's philosophies and temptations, it becomes apparent that they have been living off of Mom and Dad's faith, and they soon discover a lot of great-sounding ideas and plenty of other ways to cope with life that seem much more enjoyable. In reality, they don't possess a genuine Christian worldview that informs their basic beliefs about reality and morality.

So why do teens who seem to have all the tools needed to thrive as followers of Christ fail to filter their choices through God's Word? Why does their Christianity disconnect from the world they face every day? And what does family life have to do with all of this?

The Usual Suspects

Like runners passing the baton in an Olympic relay, we cannot afford to fumble the task of passing truth to the next generation. Tragically, even though today's youth might keep the Christian label, their beliefs do not line up with Scripture. Only 6 percent of students attending Christian schools embrace a biblical worldview.[1] According to Lifeway Research, 70 percent of Protestant young adults exit the church between the ages of 18 and 22. About *eight million* twenty-somethings who were active churchgoers as teenagers will no longer be active in a church by their thirtieth birthday. [2]

I have witnessed young people graduate from both my youth group and their Christian walk—many of whom I viewed as leaders—and have often pondered what I could have done differently. Another Bible study series? Have I told them they should save sex till marriage? That they need to forgive and communicate with their parents? That right and wrong do exist? Maybe I don't have enough programs for every conceivable age group and need. Maybe, maybe, maybe…

Why the Home?

After close to two decades of working with young people, I know two things for certain: We cannot keep doing what we've been doing, and the home environment—good or bad—makes all the difference in a young person's life. By God's design, there's an incredible advantage in handing off our faith in the home. Parents are therefore the key ingredient in making sure the next generation "gets it" for two reasons.

It's God's Plan

The undeniable truth in Scripture is that parents have an inescapable responsibility. The clearest outline of this task is found in Deuteronomy 6:4-9:

> Hear, O Israel: The LORD our God, the LORD is one. Love the LORD your God with all your heart and with all your soul and with all your strength. These commandments that I give you today are to be upon your hearts. Impress them on your children. Talk about them when you sit at home and when you walk along the road, when you lie down and when you get up. Tie them as symbols on your hands and bind them

on your foreheads. Write them on the doorframes of your
houses and on your gates (NIV).

This passage contains two main emphases for parents: *possessing*
God's principles for themselves and then intentionally *passing* these on
to their children. Mom and Dad first have a wholehearted relationship
with God as His commands dwell in their hearts, and then they deliberately pass on a godly legacy in daily living. In short, this describes a
lifestyle of modeling and communicating. And this lifestyle includes
more than formal devotions and Bible stories—it's the intertwining
of biblical principles and a Christian worldview within the context of
life. It's pointing out the beauty of God's creation, explaining moral
principles behind family standards, critiquing the philosophy of a
movie together, praying for lost friends, and cultivating a heart-level
relationship of unconditional love where a child feels safe to share
struggles and dreams.

Sadly, too many parents today aren't modeling sound doctrine,
biblical convictions, or a joyful relationship with Christ. They aren't
opening up their hearts, demonstrating a passion for God's Word,
displaying biblical tolerance, or actively reaching the lost. And as for
the second aspect of intentionally passing on God's truth, parents
are not spending significant time with their kids. Sixty-six percent
of churched youth spend an average of less than 4.5 minutes per day
with their fathers, and 62 percent spend an average of a little more
than 8.5 minutes per day with their mothers.[3] It is simply impossible
for parents to impart God's truth with such paltry time, especially if
their kids are bombarded daily with hours of the world's philosophy
through mass media. Furthermore, church programs cannot make up
for this in weekly group meetings. The influence of a pastor or teacher
is minimal compared to the real-life lessons that go on at home. God's
plan includes a lifestyle of both quality and quantity time where moms
and dads are intentionally passing on a godly legacy and discussing
things of eternal significance.

We may be tempted to think that youth have a negative attitude regarding family time, but "The State of Our Nation's Youth" reported that if students could have one wish granted, 46 percent of them would choose to have more time to spend with their families, whereas only 27 percent would choose more money and only 14 percent would choose living in a bigger house.[4] Reinforcing this truth, a 2007 MTV survey of young people between the ages of 13 and 24 asked the open-ended question, what makes you happy? The top answer was spending time with family! Nearly three-quarters of the 1280 youth surveyed said that their relationship with their parents makes them happy.[5]

The Home Is the Actual Learning Center—Good or Bad

"More is caught than taught." One of the implications of this expression is that we communicate what we actually believe through our choices, not just our words. When dad lets nothing get in the way of game-day preparations and doesn't mind jumping and yelling about the score, yet he won't carve out time for a 15-minute family devotion or express himself in worship, he communicates what he truly believes is important, despite what he might say. When mom spends her money on new shoes and a haircut but won't give a penny to the local crisis pregnancy center, when a son asks why Mormons are different from Christians and dad says to ask the youth pastor, when parents drop their kids off at Wednesday night youth but skip the adult Bible study going on at the same time…You get the message!

Youth don't want to just hear what their parents think about the Bible; they want to see that their beliefs truly make a difference. When a parent's faith is not a 24/7 thing, the kids get the message loud and clear: Christianity is merely a hobby that doesn't inform our values, priorities, or spending habits. This confusing sacred/secular dichotomy causes kids to compartmentalize their spiritual life and eventually outgrow a belief system that they've never seen modeled in a practical way. They still believe in a God who can come in handy now and then, but He's just not relevant to everyday life.

As you can imagine, the youth worker or Christian teacher cannot, in a group meeting, establish the same heart-level relationship God desires between parent and child. But when parents forego their responsibility and subcontract paid professionals, much more expectation is placed on these substitutes to be the primary spiritual caregivers. Some children do not have parents, Christian parents, or involved parents, but the painful problem we are addressing is that many parents would prefer to have anyone else do their God-ordained job.

What Can Be Done?

Determine the Goal

First, we need to clearly define what we're looking for. This might sound obvious, but we must honestly ask, what is a healthy Christian young person? Sadly, this often means we want kids who believe in God, act nice, and aren't pregnant, on drugs, or in jail. But is this all we want to pass on? Dr. Tim Kimmel defines true greatness as "a passionate love for Jesus Christ that shows itself in an unquenchable love and concern for others."[6] Again, we say amen to this, but what do we truly emphasize? Are we as concerned with Scripture memorization as academics? Do we get as fired up about God as we do about our child's sporting events? Are we as emphatic about studying God's Word as ballet or band practice? As excited about pursuing eternal riches as buying material things? The way we spend our time, money, and energy sends our actual message to young people.

Even the definition of a Christian home can be fuzzy. Does this mean we believe in God, pray, and go to church? Is it a list of things we don't do? Parents who are nice are not necessarily parents who are Bible-saturated, Spirit-led followers of Christ with a passion to intentionally pass on a godly heritage to their children. If we want kids who take their faith seriously and make an eternal impact on their world, we must talk about this and, most of all, model this at home. The wonderful result is that families thrive together during the week and then come to church with their tanks full rather than empty.

The Home Is the Key

Second, the home must once again become the key learning center. As we saw in Deuteronomy 6, parents must possess God's truth before they pass it on. So here's a question for parents: Do you get the gospel? Do you stand in awe that you are justified because Jesus took God's righteous wrath on your behalf? Do your kids know your story of how God rescued you? Are you ensuring that their children understand what Christianity is all about? Josh McDowell has made this observation:

> The majority of our young people lack a relationship with spiritual mentors who are models of Christ-likeness, and these youth are building their faith and lives on a false foundation—a distorted view of who Christ is, why He came to earth, and what the Bible and truth really are. And that has completely falsified the intent and purpose of Christianity.[7]

Parents must therefore deliberately make time to mentor their children, talking about practical Christian living and topics of eternal significance. The impact of this kind of healthy family life was underscored by the Barna Group following a 2006 survey of "tweens" (8- to 12-year-olds):

> Much of the stability and security that tweens experience is a result of their family environment and relationships...There are a variety of areas in which that experience is a struggle, but parents must be encouraged to devote themselves to investing themselves in their relationship with their children, and in providing places and opportunities for their children to mature...Parents must take the lead in establishing the centrality of faith experiences and practices for their children. That begins with parents modeling the significance of faith in their lives. It also highlights the importance of families taking the lead in the spiritual development process, rather than expecting or waiting for a church to produce spiritual growth in adolescents.[8]

I realize that many adults don't have a clear picture of this because it wasn't modeled for them and isn't a hot topic in churches. Still, each of us must look for teachable moments and create opportunities to intentionally pass on our faith. Take time to explain why Jesus is our only hope or the moral principles behind rules that apply to daily situations. This can have a powerful influence on a teenager. Maybe you need to get up to speed on current issues like postmodernism or stem-cell research. Maybe you need to set aside one night a week for family devotions and catechism. (Yes, I said catechism. Look it up!)

When the movie *Expelled: No Intelligence Allowed* came out, I used it as an opportunity for worldview training with my three oldest boys. I spent some time clarifying what evolution and Intelligent Design are all about, and then I took them to see the movie. Our family has also created some great memories helping an elderly neighbor move, going on a mission trip together, and sharing our lives with people from other walks of life that God brings across our path.

Dads Who Lead

Third, dads must take the lead! Ephesians 6:4 commands dad to deliberately train and instruct his children. Psalm 78:1-8 describes fathers and grandfathers making a successful handoff by declaring God's praiseworthy deeds, thus ensuring that His moral principles are continually passed to each succeeding generation. Dads, don't feel you have to know it all. If your child asks something you don't know, search the Scriptures, ask God for wisdom, talk to mature believers, and pray with your family. If you're not sure how to lead family devotions, do whatever it takes to find godly resources.[9] Above all, make the time and share your heart. This demonstrates humility and communicates what's important (as in, eternally important!). Satan's lie is that you are not qualified to teach your child in these areas. But the truth is that God has given you everything you need (2 Peter 3:3-4), including the grace to be the right kind of parent for your child (2 Corinthians 9:8).

The Church Can Help

Fourth, our churches must rethink the emphasis and structure of our programs. If we keep doing what we've been doing, we'll keep getting what we've been getting! Our churches need to provide ongoing training for men to lead their homes and must create opportunities for family unity and heart-level relationships. (We say family unity is important, but virtually every program splits families up.) The biblical model shows families worshipping and studying God's Word together, but we rarely provide opportunities for those who are older and wiser in the faith to pass on a clear, spiritual legacy to the next generation.[10]

Children or Young Adults?

Perhaps the most radical and yet effective step is to rethink the way we view young people and run youth ministry. I experienced a stunning revelation when I realized that our modern concepts of adolescence and teen rebellion were based on humanistic philosophy. Before you scoff and skip to the next chapter, let me explain.

From the beginning of history until about 100 years ago, teenagers were regarded in all world cultures not as children in their final phase of childhood, but as adults in their early years of adulthood (the Jewish barmitzvah, for example, emphasizes this). But in the early 1900s, Dr. G. Stanley Hall, an avid Darwinist, wanted to implement evolutionary concepts into his field of psychology. He believed that humans continue to follow the evolutionary pattern of development after birth and that the adolescent years were the final step in the process of becoming fully human and moving evolution to the next stage. Therefore, he taught that teenagers should be separated from other age groups. He also believed that because each generation is superior to the previous one, teenagers' destiny is to rebel and break free from those who preceded them.

As this way of isolating teenagers became more and more accepted in schools and churches, we essentially categorized them as a whole new class of people. Note that this method of splitting up by age was an application of evolutionary principles, not the biblical pattern of younger generations gleaning from older. Scripture actually presents the young adult years as warrior years (1 John 2:12-14), when young people don't have the distractions of spouses to care for and thus are most available for ministry (1 Corinthians 7:32).

Separating teens from adults in almost every church setting reinforces this subculture, where they are still children rather than young adults called to impact this world in the prime of their life. Constant promotion of youth-centered activities also distracts them from seeking maturity because the emphasis is mostly on Christianity being fun and cool, thus feeding what I call the hakuna matata mentality of self-indulgence and immaturity. Teens, like everyone else, should instead make the most of every opportunity (Ephesians 5:15-16) and move on to maturity (Hebrews 6:1). They think they'll get serious about God when they grow up (a vague age that gets pushed further and further back). This produces a consumer mind-set that Christianity is all about me and what I can get out of it.

The truth is that Christ calls us to die to ourselves daily, to stand for Him even if no one else does, to study His Word, and to live radically pure lives in a world obsessed with sex and self-gratification. But when a young person believes life is all about fun and feeling good, following Christ isn't too enticing. It's easier to remain a passive pewwarmer. This explains why so many youth who graduate from high school drop out of church. *Suddenly church isn't fun anymore. Suddenly everyone wants me to grow up and feed myself spiritually. If it's up to me, I'll choose the path of least resistance.*

Don't get me wrong—not all youth activities are fruitless. But the typical fluff of youth ministry runs counter to the biblical pattern of raising up next-generation Christians.

Doubts and Questions

Finally, both home and church must equip in solid doctrine, apologetics, and biblical morality. Young people consistently show signs of what I call Thomasphobia—the fear of doubting. Doubting Thomas is condemned every Easter for wanting evidence to back up his faith (even though none of the disciples believed at first). As a result, children often begin to think they're sinning if they ask hard questions about their faith. If they are not encouraged to express their doubts, one of two things could happen, both of which are grave: Either they will suppress all questions and adopt a blind faith, or they will be easily swayed by fine-sounding yet false arguments against Christianity and end up with a dead faith. They should be encouraged to question their faith as long as they maintain the right attitude and focus on the goal of discovering truth (not just a philosophy that lets them live the way they want). Teens are not losing their faith when they question basic beliefs; their faith is actually becoming their *own* faith! Wrestling with tough issues while being allowed to ask penetrating questions is a perfect way for a young person's faith to be guided and strengthened. With this in mind, here are three final things families and churches must do.

Educate in Sound Doctrine and Clear Thinking

When *Newsweek* and *Beliefnet* asked 1004 Americans, "Can a good person who doesn't share your religious beliefs attain salvation or go to heaven?" 68 percent of evangelical protestants said yes![11] This illustrates the key role of accurately teaching what Christianity is essentially about, why it is true, and why other faiths aren't. Churchgoers today are amazingly ignorant about foundational Christian beliefs and why they matter, due mainly to their lack of personal Bible study and the tendency of churches to emphasize life-enhancement principles over biblical exposition and doctrine. As a result, Christians don't see the big deal about Scripture being infallible, Jesus being sinless, or God knowing everything.

The role of the mind in the life of a Christian is essential in Bible study, spiritual growth, and taking captive false ideas (2 Corinthians 10:3-5) without becoming captive (Colossians 2:8). Often the humanistic professors in the college classroom use faulty arguments that our students have simply never heard before but that could be detected by an informed believer. Here's what one student wrote to me from college:

> I am pretty much just confused. I've been taking many science classes such as biology, geology, and archeology…It's just that I didn't expect these people to have so many answers and make it sound so smart. In church it seems like we make it out that these scientists are just making up stuff with no scientific reasoning whatsoever…I didn't expect it to sound like it made sense.

This leads us to our next step:

Equip in Apologetics

As we have already seen in previous chapters, apologetics provides the basis of a well-placed faith (1 Corinthians 15:14-17). Unfortunately, young believers don't see the importance of being able to defend their faith and to offer compelling reasons for Christianity. Eighty-four percent of first-year Christian college students cannot intelligently defend or explain their beliefs.[12] They often become interested in apologetics only in a crisis—perhaps they must finally face their doubts, or they may befriend someone of another religion. They must understand that faith is not belief in *spite* of the evidence, that believing does not make something true, and that sincerity is not all that counts. Biblical faith is trusting in what you have reason to believe is true, which makes the *object* of your faith what really matters.

If properly equipped with solid beliefs, our students will be armed with confident, ready answers (Colossians 4:5-6). After I responded to his e-mail, the student referred to earlier sent this reply:

> Thanks, that really does help a lot. I am just excited to finally be getting some real answers! It seems like so many people today plead blind faith. I would talk to other people at church and ask them if they could tell me about how Noah and the ark could have actually taken place. And someone actually

told me that "sometimes you just have to believe anyways." And I was thinking that was the last thing I wanted to hear. We shouldn't just blindly believe in something.

Explain Moral Principles

Because we want so badly for our young people to live pure lives, we often bypass the foundational step of explaining the moral principles behind God's commands and showing how these reflect His character. Abortion is wrong, but what gives human life value? Premarital sex is wrong, but what if we know we'll get married? Teens might have the right answers and even be able to give Bible verses to back them up, but they must grasp the reasons why God says things are the way they are. We must clearly communicate that our choices reveal what we truly believe about God, His Word, and His plan for our lives (Titus 1:16).

God has provided every parent with a home-field advantage when it comes to training and equipping the next wave of Christ followers. There is hope for future generations when Mom and Dad understand and possess God's life-changing truth, model Jesus to their kids in everyday life through godly attitudes and actions, and intentionally pass on biblical principles in the context of heart-level relationships. What a blessing and privilege to inspire lives of obedience, love, and service that will outlast this life!

Chris Sherrod is a pastor, Bible teacher, speaker, and author, and now works with Pine Cove Christian Camps as director of The Bluffs family camp.

Part 3

NEW CHALLENGES

The election of 2008 was historic. With the unprecedented election of an African-American for president of the United States, race has been jettisoned back into the center of cultural conversation. To effectively minister to a new generation, Christians must be prepared to address racial issues with compassion, clarity, and accuracy.

As an American with Indian descent, Alison Thomas offers an important encouragement and admonition for the contemporary church in her chapter, "Race and Apologetics." According to Thomas, our culturally pluralistic world demands that we strive for racial diversity, reconciliation, and balanced representation within the church.

But race is not the only new challenge facing our emerging generation. Issues such as homosexuality, gender, abortion, and the identity of Jesus continue to be at the forefront of our cultural conversation. Sadly, many outsiders view the Christian church as dominated by males and as oppressive to females. In her chapter, "Defending Feminity," Jonalyn Fincher demonstrates how Jesus, more than any other religious figure, can make a real life-changing difference to women today.

Each of the remaining chapters is written by a young leader who has his or her pulse on contemporary culture. We must rethink how to freshly engage the new challenges that are arising for this generation.

Sean McDowell

JESUS:
RISEN FOR A NEW GENERATION

by Jason Carlson

always enjoy seeing whom I'll end up sitting next to when I'm traveling on an airplane. On one recent trip from Minneapolis to Seattle, I had a very interesting encounter.

When Matt sat down next to me, I was immediately intrigued. He looked to be about my age, probably in his late twenties or early thirties, but Matt definitely didn't look like me. Matt was a stereotypical young, postmodern, urban hipster—part punk and part Goth with a healthy dose of metrosexual thrown in. He had that perfect blend of being mysterious, but not outright scary. His arms were tattooed, his ears and an eyebrow were pierced, his hair was messy (the kind of messy that requires a lot of gel and attention to detail), and he wore stylish jeans and a blazer jacket with a vintage T-shirt underneath.

As our flight got underway, and after some brief introductions, I noticed Matt pull out a book from his messenger bag, and the title immediately caught my attention. It was a book on Eastern and Buddhist philosophy. Of course, I was intrigued. I have been formally trained in philosophy and have spent most of my adult life traveling around the world studying and ministering to people caught up in false religious philosophies, so I simply couldn't help but ask Matt about his current reading selection.

During a pause from his reading, I turned to Matt and said to him, "Excuse me, but I happened to notice the book you're reading. If you don't mind my asking…what drew you to a book on Eastern philosophy?" Matt then explained to me that he was currently taking a college course on Buddhism, but then he went on to offer that this course was simply one piece of a quest for truth that he had recently embarked on, a quest that had led him toward the study of the world's major religions and philosophies. You can imagine what I was feeling inside.

Bridges for the Gospel

As a pastor and a teacher, I regularly encourage people to look for bridges for the gospel. A bridge is simply a ready-made opportunity that lends itself toward a spiritual conversation through which we believers might share the truth about Christ and the hope that is found in Him. And as I often tell people, these bridges are all around us, all the time. We just need to have eyes to see them and the boldness, passion, and faith to use them when they present themselves.

So here I was, a pastor and Christian apologist, sitting next to another young man who by his own admission was longing to know the truth about the ultimate questions of life.[1] Talk about a bridge for sharing the gospel! I quickly said a silent prayer, and then I began to share some of my personal testimony with Matt.

For the next two hours, Matt and I had a truly engaging, passionate, and honest conversation about a whole variety of spiritual topics. We were both filled with energy, but neither of us became aggressive or hostile. Matt was truly hungry for answers, and I thoroughly enjoyed his openness, his appreciative spirit, and his obvious grasp of many of the religious and philosophical concepts we talked about—even though we didn't see eye to eye on a number of them.

Why Christ?

Matt asked me one question that I have mulled over in my mind numerous times since then. At one point in our conversation Matt looked me dead in the eyes and asked me point-blank, "Jason, tell me something—what's your bottom line? When you boil it all down, why are you a Christian?"

As I sat there on the plane that day, quickly reviewing in my mind the numerous reasons I could share with Matt for why I've placed my trust in Jesus Christ, suddenly one word impressed itself upon my thoughts—"resurrection." Without hesitation I said, "Matt, my bottom line is very simple. I am a Christian for a number of reasons, but at the end of the day, if there is one primary reason for why I've chosen to follow Jesus Christ, it is that He is a living Savior. Jesus was not simply a great religious teacher. Rather, He claimed to be God in human flesh, the Messiah or Savior of the world, and He verified these claims by conquering sin and death when He rose from the grave. In one word, Matt, I'm a Christian because of Jesus' resurrection."

This response definitely piqued Matt's curiosity. And he said to me with full sincerity, "But you don't really believe Jesus literally rose from the dead, do you?" And with this question I spent the remainder of our flight walking Matt through the compelling evidence for the historical reality of Jesus Christ's resurrection from the dead.

Serious Business

I began by pulling my Bible from my backpack and reading from 1 Corinthians 15:12-20.

> But if it is preached that Christ has been raised from the dead, how can some of you say that there is no resurrection of the dead? If there is no resurrection of the dead, then not even Christ has been raised. And if Christ has not been raised, our preaching is useless and so is your faith. More than that, we are then found to be false witnesses about God, for we have testified about God that he raised Christ from the dead. But he did not raise him if in fact the dead are not raised. For if the dead are not raised, then Christ has not been raised either. And if Christ has not been raised, your faith is futile; you are still in your sins. Then those also who have fallen asleep

in Christ are lost. If only in this life we have hope in Christ, we are to be pitied more than all men. But Christ has indeed been raised from the dead, the firstfruits of those who have fallen asleep (NIV).

After reading this passage, I said, "You see, Matt, for Christians, our entire faith rests on the claim that Jesus Christ was physically resurrected from the grave. Even the earliest followers of Jesus recognized this. As the apostle Paul says here, if Jesus didn't truly rise from the grave, our faith is 'useless' and 'futile.' And the 'futile' part here is especially significant because if Jesus didn't really rise from the grave, He was just another guy crucified by the Romans on a cross, and we then have no forgiveness for sins or any hope for eternal life. If the resurrection didn't happen, I might as well pack it up and go home. Christianity stands or falls on the historical reality of the resurrection of Jesus Christ."

Before I could go any further, Matt was already connecting the dots and was one step ahead of me. "So how do you know Jesus really did rise from the dead?"

Now I was getting really excited because I love talking about the evidence for the resurrection of Jesus Christ. And I believe that a very convincing case can be made for the historic Christian claim that Jesus physically rose from the grave and conquered sin and death.

No Silver Bullets in Apologetics

However, before I move on to what I shared with Matt, let me simply offer a brief comment on the nature of Christian apologetics. When I teach on apologetics, I often find that many Christians are looking for a silver bullet, an argument that will convince every skeptic, defeat every critique, or win every debate. But as I regularly share with these people, no such silver bullet exists.

Instead, we should probably view Christian apologetics more like a toolbox. And within our toolbox we have a number of very helpful resources at our disposal. Sometimes one individual apologetic argument will win the heart and mind of the skeptic, critic, or non-believer, but usually you'll need a variety of apologetic tools to help the person you're sharing with. No one argument for the resurrection will win over every skeptic, but when taken as a whole, the evidence for Jesus' resurrection becomes very compelling.

A Compelling Case

In response to Matt's question, I began to share with him some of what I believe to be the most persuasive arguments for the historical credibility of the resurrection of Jesus Christ. We talked about the fact that Jesus truly died, that He didn't swoon or slip into a coma, and that nobody was secretly substituted in His place. I shared with Matt the powerful testimony of the empty tomb, that three days after his execution and burial, Jesus' tomb was dramatically opened, and his body was no longer there. Jews, Romans, and Christians all agreed on this fact. I highlighted the remarkable accounts of the eyewitness testimonies to the risen Jesus and how Scripture reveals that more than 500 people saw and physically experienced the resurrected Christ. We talked about the powerful impact these experiences had on people's lives throughout Jerusalem and Israel, along with the implications of these eyewitness testimonies for the rapid spread of the early church in the hostile climate of first-century Israel. And lastly, Matt and I discussed the testimonies of people's lives that were dramatically changed as a result of witnessing Jesus' resurrection, including the disciples, Jesus' half-brother James, and the apostle Paul, who was once a zealous Jewish persecutor of the early Christian church. Matt seemed especially impressed when he found out that all of these people went to their deaths, all but one as martyrs, convinced of the fact and unwilling to deny that Jesus truly was the resurrected Messiah.

Before we knew it our flight landed in Seattle, and unfortunately, Matt and I were just getting warmed up! We'd had a wonderful conversation for more than two hours, and I could tell that Matt's heart was truly open to the Lord.

The Power of Resurrection Apologetics

Since that day, Matt and I have maintained a regular e-mail dialogue and have further developed our friendship. As of this writing, I don't believe Matt has yet chosen to follow Jesus Christ as his Lord and Savior, but I really think he's close! And Matt has told me numerous times that what impresses him the most about the claims of the Christian faith are the arguments for the resurrection of Jesus Christ. As Matt recently told me, "Out of all the great religious teachers in the history of the world, only Jesus Christ made the types of claims He did about Himself. And only the followers of Jesus have dared to claim that their teacher conquered death. This is what intrigues me most about Jesus."

Matt's story highlights the power of the case for the resurrection of Jesus Christ in reaching the postmodern world. The emerging generations today, both within and outside the church, desperately need to hear this case. They need to be taught that the resurrection is more than just a cool story about a 2000-year-old event that we commemorate on Easter Sunday. They need to hear the compelling evidence for the resurrection, and they need to hear that it means something for them today!

Does It Really Matter?

Recently a young woman named Amy came to me with some questions she'd been pondering as a result of a lecture she had heard in one of our local universities. Apparently she was enrolled in a course that was examining the Bible as literature. And as it turned out, a large portion of this class was being devoted to challenging the integrity of the Bible's accounts of various historical events, including Jesus' resurrection.

As this young collegian reflected on her faith and what she had been hearing in her class, she soon found herself wrestling with a very profound question: What difference does it make if Jesus' resurrection was literally true or not? And as she shared this question with me recently over a cup of coffee she added, "I mean, does it really matter?

What if Jesus didn't rise from the dead? What if the story was just made up? Does that really change the power and significance of what Jesus taught and how He lived?"

If Amy had brought these questions to you, what would you have told her? What can we share with twenty-first-century young people today about the meaning of Jesus' resurrection for them? What difference does the literal, historical resurrection of Christ make for younger generations?

The Life-Transforming Power of the Resurrection

As I sat with Amy in our local coffee shop, I knew that there was life-transforming power in the truth of Jesus' resurrection, and I desperately wanted her to see this too. I started out by saying, "Amy, the historical reality of Jesus' resurrection makes all the difference in the world." And I went on to highlight the following points.

The Resurrection Proves the Deity and Lordship of Jesus Christ

Apart from His resurrection from the dead, Jesus was at best a great teacher of morality, maybe even the greatest, but that's it. If Jesus did not rise from the grave, today He lies buried alongside all the other great philosophers and religious teachers throughout the history of the world. No Son of God. No Messiah. No returning King.

However, the apostle Paul tells us in Romans 1:4 that Jesus was "declared with power to be the Son of God by his resurrection from the dead" (NIV). At this point I said to Amy, "Many people have claimed to be divine, many have claimed to know the way to salvation, but not many people have claimed these things and then verified their claims by rising from the grave!" As Thomas Oden puts it, "There is no direct parallel in the history of religions of a founder whose bodily resurrection from the dead confirms and ratifies his life and teaching."[2]

It's because of His resurrection from the dead that we believe Jesus' remarkable claims about Himself: that He is the eternal Son of God who is "the way, the truth, and the life" (John 14:6). And it's because of Jesus' resurrection that we can confidently put our trust in Him as the Lord of our lives, living for Him, serving Him, and watching expectantly for His triumphal return.

The Resurrection Guarantees Our Personal Salvation

"Do you believe you are saved? If so, why?" These were the questions I posed to Amy as I came to this second point in our conversation. As is common for most Christian young people, Amy said she believed she was saved because "Jesus died for my sins and I've put my faith in Him."

I replied, "So what? People put their faith in lots of things. Why do you think putting your faith in Jesus is so special?"

This question might sound pretty harsh, but this is something we need to seriously challenge Christian young people to consider. Why do we put our faith in Jesus Christ? Why not Buddha? Reincarnation? Muhammad? Or even the Easter Bunny? The point our young people need to grasp is that our faith in Jesus Christ only means something because Jesus Christ is a living Savior! The only reason we have any hope for salvation by faith in Jesus Christ is that Jesus not only died on a cross for our sins but also verified the efficacy of His death for us by conquering the grave.

In Romans 4:25 the apostle Paul reports that Jesus "was delivered over to death for our sins and was raised to life for our justification" (NIV). What is justification? "Justification" is a word that brings to mind the image of standing in a courtroom, guilty in the eyes of the law, awaiting your sentence. Yet as you stand there, another person suddenly walks into the courtroom and says, "I will serve her sentence in her place." And with that the judge reports that you are free to go—the penalty has been taken away from you.

Isn't that amazing? Jesus died for our sins, in our place, but as the apostle Paul says, it is because Jesus was raised to life that we are justified, pardoned, and forgiven in the eyes of God. The apostle Peter echoes this truth when he writes in 1 Peter 1:3, "Praise be to the God and Father of our Lord Jesus Christ! In his great mercy he has given us new birth into a living hope through the resurrection of Jesus Christ from the dead" (NIV).

Notice the significance that both Paul and Peter place on Jesus' resurrection from the dead, directly connecting the resurrection to our personal salvation. As I said earlier, many Christian young people today are quick to point to Jesus' death on the cross and their faith in Him as the reason for their salvation. And yet this is only half of the story. If those of us who are Christian educators and ministers to those in the emerging generations of the church fail to emphasize the centrality of the resurrection event, we are failing to give our Christian young people a full, biblical understanding of our salvation, which comes through Jesus Christ.

The Resurrection Guarantees Our Future Resurrection and Eternal Life with God

In my opinion, this is the most exciting reality of the resurrection. As I shared this truth with Amy that day, I did so with the knowledge that Amy was still grieving the loss of her grandfather, who had passed away only a few weeks earlier. Amy's grandfather was a great man, a godly man, and a respected leader in his church for many years. Knowing that Amy sat there with a heavy heart, I said, "Amy, can I show you two of the most exciting verses in all of Scripture?" And with that I opened my Bible and read for her from John 11:25-26: "Jesus said to her, 'I am the resurrection and the life; he who believes in me will live even if he dies, and everyone who lives and believes in Me will never die.'"

After reading this passage I said, "Amy, your grandfather put his trust in Jesus Christ as his Lord and Savior. And because of this, Jesus says that your grandfather would never die."

As she thought about this, for a moment Amy's lips briefly curled up into a smile, but then she asked somewhat somberly, "But how can that be?"

I replied, "Well, wait a minute. It gets more exciting!" And I turned to 2 Corinthians 5:1-2 and read: "Now we know that if the earthly tent we live in is destroyed, we have a building from God, an eternal house in heaven, not built by human hands. Meanwhile we groan, longing to be clothed with our heavenly dwelling" (NIV).

I stopped here and explained to Amy, "Now, the Bible describes this physical body of ours as a temporary dwelling or house that our soul lives in. If you read 2 Corinthians 4, you'll see that Paul calls the body an 'earthen vessel.' It's only temporary." I then turned to 2 Corinthians 5:8 and read, "We are confident, I say, and would prefer to be away from the body and at home with the Lord" (NIV).

"You see, Amy," I continued, "for the Christian, to be absent from this physical body is not something we should fear. Rather, when believers pass away, their souls leave their bodies, and they instantaneously go to be at home with the Lord. How do I know this? Because of what we just read a minute ago, where Jesus said, 'I am the resurrection and the life. If you believe in me, you shall never die.' And why won't believers, like your grandfather, ever die? Because when you accept Jesus Christ as your personal Lord and Savior, He comes to live within you. And in living within you, Jesus empowers you with His Holy Spirit and gives to you His resurrection power." I could tell that Amy was starting to see it now, the life-transforming power found in the truth of Jesus' resurrection, and so I added, "Amy, believe it or not, it gets even more exciting!" And I turned in my Bible to Philippians 1:21 where the apostle Paul says: "For to me, to live is Christ and to die is gain."

I then asked Amy, "Why would Paul say that 'to die is gain'?"

By this point Amy had totally gotten it. "Because for a believer, to be absent from the body is to be at home with the Lord," she said. And then, as if to just make sure that I knew she got it, she added, "Because Jesus said, 'I am the resurrection and life. If you believe in me, you shall never die.'" Amy's spirit had visibly changed by this point in our conversation. It appeared that her doubts and sadness had been lifted and totally replaced by the knowledge that Jesus truly is the risen Prince of Peace.

This is the great hope that we as believers have as a result of Jesus' resurrection from the dead—we need not fear death. Jesus has already defeated death! He is a risen Savior. And when people put their trust in Jesus Christ as their Savior and Lord, they immediately receive Jesus' resurrection power in their own lives. This is why the apostle Paul could so confidently declare that to be absent from the body is to be at home with the Lord. This is also why Paul could so boldly taunt death in 1 Corinthians 15:55, where he says, "Where, O death, is your victory? Where, O death, is your sting?" (NIV).

The Shadow of Death

A close family friend of ours, my father's mentor and teacher, was the late Dr. Walter Martin. He was a pioneer in the field of Christian apologetics and especially in the areas of cults and non-Christian philosophies. In fact, he wrote the classic book *The Kingdom of the Cults.* Dr. Martin's mentor and teacher was the late great theologian Dr. Donald Grey Barnhouse, and Dr. Martin used to share a powerful story from Dr. Barnhouse's life.

Dr. Barnhouse's wife had passed away, and he and his young daughter were driving together to her funeral service. As they were driving, Dr. Barnhouse was trying to figure out how to explain to his daughter what death was. And as he was sharing with her, he quoted from Psalm 23 and then began to try and explain what David meant when he said, "Even though I walk through the valley of the shadow of death, I fear no evil." Have you ever wondered what that verse means? Why does David refer to the "valley of the shadow of death"?

Dr. Barnhouse was trying to explain that to his daughter as they came to a stoplight. The day was bright and sunny, and while they were waiting at the stoplight, a large truck pulled up next to them. The truck blocked the sun and cast a huge shadow over their car. When this happened, Dr. Barnhouse asked his daughter, "Tell me something, would you rather be hit by the truck or the shadow of the truck?"

She said, "Well, I'd rather be hit by the shadow of the truck."

Dr. Barnhouse replied, "That's exactly what David means when he says, 'Though I walk through the valley of the shadow of death, I will fear no evil.'"

Jesus Christ took the hit of death for us when he died on the cross of Calvary. Believers, therefore, do not face death. We face the shadow of death but not death itself. As we saw earlier, for the Christian, to be absent from the body is to be immediately at home with the Lord. And as Paul says, "For to me, to live is Christ and to die is gain" (Philippians 1:21). For the believer in Jesus Christ, death is only a shadow; it has lost its sting! Because of Jesus' resurrection, believers can be confident that we too will rise again. The grave held no power over Jesus Christ, and it holds no power over those who've put their trust in Him.

The Gospel for a New Generation

The story of Jesus' death and resurrection has been the cornerstone of the church for more than 2000 years. And the reality of Jesus' life, death, and resurrection from the grave has been a source of hope for countless millions of people. No other person in history has had a greater transformational affect on humanity than Jesus Christ. His influence far exceeds any other force that has ever been felt on earth.

This is why the story of Jesus' life has come to be known as the gospel. What does the word "gospel" mean? It means "good news." And the historical reality of Jesus' life, His death, and especially His resurrection from the grave is very good news. It's good news for a world that is desperately searching for something to believe in. It's good news for all who are hurting and without hope. It's been good news for countless millions for more than 2000 years, and it is the good news we have to offer the emerging generations today.

Jesus Christ is the risen Savior of the postmodern world. We do not offer emerging generations the sayings of a long-deceased sage or the model of a saint. We offer them the risen King of kings and Lord of lords. Jesus Christ alone has the power to save us from our sins.

He alone has the power to transform people's lives. This is the gospel. And this gospel is as relevant and necessary today for a new generation as it ever has been.

Jason Carlson is the vice president of Christian Ministries International, an associate pastor in New Brighton, MN, and an adjunct faculty member at Bethel Seminary and North-western College.

APOLOGETICS AND RACE

by Alison Thomas

The glittering threads of race and ethnicity have always been inextricably woven throughout the fabric of my faith. I was born and raised in the United States to first-generation immigrants from India. My parents both grew up in vibrant, charismatic Christian homes in Kerala, a state located in the southern part of India.

Tradition holds that the apostle Thomas brought Christianity to India in the first century and established a church there that remains to this day. Several notable early church fathers and historians including Eusebius of Caesarea, Ambrose of Milan, and Gregory of Nazianzus have made reference to Thomas going to India, and there is no compelling evidence to the contrary.

In the city of Chennai is a hilltop church called St. Thomas Mount that is believed to be the place where Thomas was martyred. Christians in India whose traditions flow from this early church are popularly known as "St. Thomas Christians" and also as "Syrian Christians" because the liturgy used since the early days is in Syriac, a classical form of Aramaic.

Finding out that my ancestors were born in the shadow of the "Doubting Apostle" himself has had a profound impact on my life. Over the years I've developed a deep empathy for the apostle because of his work in India, and also because I have always been a doubting Thomas of sorts myself, which is what led me into the field of Christian apologetics. Apologetics for a new generation must be conversant with the complex racial and cultural nuances of the worldwide church in order to have an impact today.

Christianity and Imperialism

Christianity is alleged to be today's greatest enemy of diversity and multiculturalism. It is often characterized as an invasive Western tradition that goes out into the world and dominates other cultures, stripping them of their uniqueness and innocence. It is also seen as an enemy within America, dividing what would be an otherwise united people. A fashionable slogan often uttered by American young people is, "How can you think your culture's perspective is the only one that's right? That is so arrogant and narrow-minded!" People of different backgrounds are often surprised that I am of Indian descent and a Christian. Americans are stunned to hear that not all Indians are Hindu. Indians themselves are shocked to hear that Christianity has had a long history in India and was not solely the result of colonial imposition.

Can we deny that imperialism, racism, sexism, and all sorts of oppression have been spread in the name of Christianity and in religion in general? Sadly, we cannot. But eradicating religion does not guarantee the end of violence. Much bloodshed has been carried out by secularist regimes led by the likes of Stalin, Mao, and Pol Pot. Christianity today is more peaceful that it has been in the past, while other worldviews continue in their violence. Hindu extremists today carry out bloody assaults on both Christian churches and Muslim mosques. People often try to equate today's Islamic fundamentalism with Christian fundamentalism, but they have yet to find the Christian al-Qaeda, the Christian Hamas, or the Christian Hezbollah. In their desperate and strained attempts to portray modern Christianity as a religion of violence, skeptics present certain marginal individuals as being representative of the faith even though such ideas are not compatible with the teachings of Jesus or practiced by most Christians today.

Christianity and Diversity

Throughout its history, Christianity has actually been more

representative and inclusive of diverse cultures than many other world-views. Timothy Keller explains:

> The original lands that have been the demographic centers of Hinduism, Buddhism, and Confucianism have remained so. By contrast, Christianity was first dominated by Jews and centered in Jerusalem. Later it was dominated by Hellenists and centered in the Mediterranean. Later the faith was received by the barbarians of Northern Europe and Christianity came to be dominated by western Europeans and then North Americans.[1]

Today, more than two out of three evangelical Christians live in Asia, Africa, or South America. The largest Christian congregation in the world, the Yoido Full Gospel Church, is located in South Korea and has more than 800,000 members. South Korea sends out the world's second largest number of Christian missionaries. China could possibly boast the largest Christian population in the world in just a few decades. Nearly 50 percent of the African population is Christian today. In 1900, it was only 9 percent. African scholar Lamin Sanneh describes one of the reasons why Christianity is spreading so rapidly in Africa:

> People sensed in their hearts that Jesus did not mock their respect for the sacred nor their clamor for an invincible savior, and so they beat their sacred drums for him until the stars skipped and danced in the skies...Christianity helped Africans to become renewed Africans, not re-made Europeans.[2]

Sanneh says that a worldview like secularism, because of its antisupernaturalism and individualism, is much more damaging to diversity and "African-ness" than Christianity is. Interestingly enough, this explosive growth of Christianity in the developing world began after the days of European colonialism ended.

The New Face of the Global Church

Christianity is not a Western religion. It did not originate in the

West, nor is it centered in the West today. Contrary to what many people think, the truly representative face of today's Christianity is not that of a white American man. Philip Jenkins says, "If we want to visualize a typical contemporary Christian, we should think of a woman living in a village in Nigeria or in a Brazilian favela."[3]

Although the West was the driving force of the church in the world at one time, this is clearly no longer the case. Some say that today, the United States is one of the largest unreached nations in the world with the authentic gospel. Just because we can produce extravagant events and sell massive amounts of Christian products doesn't mean we are living out our faith more deeply and having more impact in the world than Christians in poorer countries. Dinesh D'Souza paints an interesting picture:

> At one time Christian missionaries went to the far continents of Africa and Asia, where white priests in robes proclaimed the Bible to wide-eyed and uncomprehending brown and black people. In the future, we may well see black and brown missionaries proclaim the Bible to wide-eyed and uncomprehending white people in the West.[4]

Multiculturalism and the American Church

Maintaining unity amid diversity within the church provides a crucial witness to the power of the gospel. Such an accomplishment would be a most powerful apologetic for a new generation. In America, the rapid growth of diverse racial and cultural groups has created dramatic tensions within the church. An important distinction needs to be made here between race and culture. Race is biological; culture is environmental. You cannot change your race, but you can change your culture. Every culture has aspects that can be critiqued and corrected by Christianity. Not so with race, as Ravi Zacharias writes:

> Race is a very sacred thing. It is the gift of God to each individual. It is something in which we had no choice or say. We were born with our ethnicity; it is not a culturally assigned

quality. Therefore, it should never be violated...Are all races equal? Yes. But are there differences? Absolutely. Do those differences make it one's right to dominate the other? No.[5]

For me, straddling two different cultures while growing up was rich, complex, and contradictory. I attended a White Southern Baptist school during the week and an Indian pentecostal church on the weekends. What I always found most confusing as a child was not the glaring theological differences between denominations, but the way in which Christian leaders on both sides constantly misrepresented the faith of the other culture.

How should we as Christians in America respond to our racial and cultural diversity? The book *United by Faith* makes a bold and controversial argument: "Christian congregations, when possible, should be multiracial...This conclusion rests in part on the premise that multiracial congregations can play an important role in reducing racial division and inequality and that this should be a goal of Christian people."[6]

The growing number of interracial marriages and multiracial children in America shows that cultural pluralism is not an issue the American church can ignore. Many American evangelicals see cultural pluralism as the same as religious pluralism and reject it because it seems too politically correct to embrace. As believers, we are called to respect people's cultures while we engage with their religious ideas. We can keep people in equality while we put ideas in hierarchy. Cultural pluralism does not have to denigrate into moral relativism. The book of Revelation depicts a reconciled future world in which the cultural differences of "every tongue, tribe, people, and nation" are retained. There is great blessing in striving to model such reconciliation within our churches today, even though the journey to accomplish this will be long and arduous.

The Journey to Racial Reconciliation

American evangelicalism is still dominated by white leadership, which can be alienating to some. Many second-generation, bicultural Americans find it extremely difficult to find a place within the church. I never felt comfortable in my white Christian school. But I didn't feel comfortable in my Indian church either. The services were all in Malayalam, a native Indian language that I didn't understand all that well. I had to wear heavy ethnic clothing that covered me from head to toe—long skirts, long sleeves, and a veil on my head—all in hot, humid South Florida weather.

What I also found unacceptable about the Indian church was its rejection of anything that smacked of white American Christianity. It was subtly communicated that Eastern culture was morally superior to Western culture. Easterners were perceived as less sexually promiscuous (because dating was not allowed), less likely to divorce (because marriages were arranged), and more likely to care for aging parents personally (because extended families usually lived close by). All of these ideas were propagated by a church that affirmed original sin and the depravity of *all* humanity! Perhaps the leaders within my Indian church were prejudiced toward white Christians and stayed within a close-knit Indian community because they would not be allowed positions of authority in white churches.

As long as different Christian groups refuse to interact with one another, misunderstandings and inequality will continue to be perpetuated. More and more white churches are seeing the value and importance of providing visibility to ethnic minorities who are gifted and trained for leadership. Bob Roberts elaborates on this:

> I don't think the answers to engaging our world in the future will come from old, dead, white theologians alone. Perhaps they have left us enough to begin a discussion—but trying to place their global understanding and framework of life into a twenty-first-century church will not be sufficient. It's time for new theologians. We need some new Luthers and Calvins and Zwinglis. Their names will probably be Lukito Sumatra, Phuc Dang, Akmed Muhammad, and others.[7]

Representation and Responsibility

More minorities also need to step up to the challenge by becoming cross-cultural leaders in the church rather than remaining in the comfort zones of their own ethnic enclaves. I'll never forget what I was thinking the first time I heard Ravi Zacharias speak: *Is that really an Indian accent I hear on this American Christian radio station?* He was able to connect with me and encourage me in a way no one else could. People need to see their ethnicity reflected in their Christian leadership. This is why I now speak to young people all over the world. I want to do for them what Ravi did for me. The cultural consciousness and racial reconciliation that apologetics for a new generation requires will not happen on its own. Each of us has to do our part by taking risks and being open to possible rejection in order to further change.

The future of Christianity in the United States depends on racial reconciliation and balanced representation within the church. The spiritual convergence of cultures is made possible through the cross of Christ, the common cord that mysteriously holds together the exquisite tapestry of our faith.

> For Christ himself has brought peace to us. He united Jews and Gentiles into one people when, in his own body on the cross, he broke down the wall of hostility that separated us. He did this by ending the system of law with its commandments and regulations. He made peace between Jews and Gentiles by creating in himself one new people from the two groups. Together as one body, Christ reconciled both groups to God by means of his death on the cross, and our hostility toward each other was put to death (Ephesians 2:14-16 NLT).

Alison Thomas is a speaker and writer with Ravi Zacharias International Ministries.

AN INTERVIEW WITH MIKE LICONA

Sean McDowell: What topics in apologetics seem to be especially relevant and important to this generation?

Mike Licona: Apologetics topics presently enjoying the most attention are relativism, the exclusivity claims of Christ, the historical Jesus—even including the question of whether He ever existed—the trustworthiness of the Bible, Islam, and New Age ideas that Oprah has brought to the forefront. I'm getting hints within the academic community that canonicity may be one of the next big topics for discussion—not necessarily whether the Gnostic literature should be included in the New Testament canon, but rather whether specific letters presently included should be, such as Hebrews, 2 Peter, 2 and 3 John, Jude, and Revelation.

Sean: Do we need to make substantial changes in our approach or content when presenting apologetics to this generation?

Mike: I think this largely depends on whom you're talking to. A majority of North Americans have very little to no knowledge of the Bible, including its characters and stories. For many, the Bible is just another holy book with no privileged position over the holy writings of Muslims and Hindus. Therefore, claiming that one should believe the Christian message because the Bible is God's Word now carries little to no weight.

Many North Americans are either modernists or postmodernists. The former place an emphasis on logic, evidence, and truth whereas the latter are more concerned with pragmatism, fairness, and even contrarianism. The former say, "You should believe X because it is true for three logical reasons." The latter say, "We all find different truths along differing routes. Can't we all just get along?"

Our approach to modernists must differ from how we approach postmodernists. To the former we must be prepared to provide evidence from science, history, and philosophy for why the Christian message provides ultimate truth about God. The latter best connect through stories to which they can relate their personal experience rather than bullet-point logic.

Sean: What advice would you give for incorporating apologetics training into the life of the church today?

Mike: There are a number of great apologetics books that will appeal to individuals on different parts of their journey. Books by Josh McDowell and Alex McFarland have a high appeal to students. Ravi Zacharias has a large appeal to abstract and postmodern thinkers. Gary Habermas and William Lane Craig appeal to modernist intellectuals. Lee Strobel and Mark Mittelberg provide excellent resources from which both modernists and postmodernists may benefit. None of us can be all things to all people, so churches can seek to identify one or more members who are passionate about apologetics, encourage and empower these to train fellow members in apologetics, and provide funding for outreach activities using apologetics.

> **Mike Licona** serves in apologetics and interfaith evangelism at the North American Mission Board in Atlanta, Georgia, and is coauthor of the 2005 award-winning book *The Case for the Resurrection of Jesus.*

HOMOSEXUALITY:
KNOW THE TRUTH AND
SPEAK IT WITH COMPASSION

by Alan Shlemon

I t's not surprising people think Christians hate homosexuals. They see the way we often treat them.

Kyle's sad story was similar to others I'd heard. After 25 years of immersion in the gay lifestyle, he wanted out. His choice to follow Jesus meant a day-to-day struggle to stay celibate because simply becoming a Christian didn't change his same-sex desires. With God's help, though, he was winning the battle.

Kyle thought his church would be a safe harbor during the storm. But when he "came out" to his pastor and a counselor, both told him to never speak of his plight again. His church forced him back into the closet.

Fifteen years of celibacy later, Kyle came out a second time. *Surely things have changed,* he thought. *It must be safe now. After all, everyone has struggles and temptations.* This time he hoped his new church would come alongside and pray for him. But he was mistaken. They turned a blind eye to his struggle, discouraged him from serving, and relegated him to attending and tithing.

Back into the Closet

Our formula for gays is predictable: Condemn and convert. Rebuke their behavior, blast them with the Bible, and then try to win them over with a cliché.[1]

"Sodomy is sin," we proclaim. Then we quote our "clobber passage," a verse that condemns homosexuals or even commands their execution.[2] "But there's hope," we reassure them. "God hates the sin but loves the sinner." That's not what they hear, though. They hear one word: "hate."

Armed with Bible verses for bullets, we're locked and loaded, ready to fire at the first sign of a homosexual. But there's no grace in a gunshot. Instead of offering hope and healing, we inflict more injury.

We shouldn't be surprised when gays go back into the closet after they try to come out in the church. Worse, many go back into the lifestyle, sometimes through a "gay church" that shows them the love, grace, and respect they had hoped to get from us.[3]

Predictably, younger people often perceive Christianity negatively. The Barna Group found that young people think Christians are not only opposed to homosexuality but also show "excessive contempt and unloving attitudes towards gays and lesbians." Ninety-one percent of young non-Christians and 80 percent of young churchgoers perceive Christianity as "anti-homosexual."[4]

More tragically, the Barna study found that younger Christians complained their church failed to help them apply biblical principles to their friendships with gays. Young people lack arguments and tactics needed to maneuver in conversation and navigate moral dilemmas in a thoughtful but loving way. Consequently, young people think they must choose between their faith and their friends who are gay. If their friendships mean more to them than their theology, they will choose their friends over their faith every time.

Something is wrong here. Clearly, we need a new approach. Our young people think they're faced with a difficult moral dilemma. But they don't have to abandon their gay friends just because homosexuality is wrong. There is a third option, but it's something that's rarely taught or modeled in church.

Know the Truth

Our new approach incorporates two key elements: truth and compassion. Truth speaks to the content of our message. Compassion addresses the manner in which it's conveyed. It's a winning combination based on principles found in 1 Peter 3:15—defend the truth with gentleness and respect.

Truth starts with a biblical understanding of homosexuality. Although there are six main passages on the subject, for strategic reasons I recommend using Romans 1:26-27 as your primary text.[5] It's in the New Testament, so you sidestep the challenge that the Old Testament verses don't apply to us today.[6] Romans also addresses both male and female homosexuality and outlines the real problem: rebellion against God and rejection of His created order. This makes it difficult to argue that the behavior condemned in the passage is something other than homosexuality.[7]

Knowing the biblical truth about homosexuality is important because many people deny that God condemns homosexual behavior. Indeed, they go to great lengths to reinterpret those six passages.[8] Although they're not successful, their claims sound appealing to people who don't carefully interpret the Bible. If we learn and understand these verses, clearing up this distortion is easy.

Religious arguments, however, are often immediately dismissed by non-Christians. So knowing the truth doesn't mean we learn only biblical arguments. An effective strategy also incorporates secular arguments. This includes appeals to natural law, the common good, and public health.[9] If you can base your views on evidence that make sense even to nonreligious people, you'll be able to speak with anyone.

Getting them to consider your ideas can be difficult though. That's why it's critical to present our views in a conversational manner. We're not typically trained to do that. Too often we try to persuade by making statements instead of asking questions. This immediately raises defenses. Suppose you're discussing whether homosexuality is genetic and say, "Even if being gay is genetic, that doesn't mean that it's right."

Your friend replies with, "Sure it does! I can't deny how I've been created." Now what? Another statement? Their defenses are up, and the conversation grinds to a halt.

Questions, on the other hand, are friendly and more engaging. They invite discussion. Rephrase your statement with a question: "I'm curious to know your thoughts on this. Can you tell me why you think if something is genetic, it must be right?" This is disarming. It doesn't provoke the same knee-jerk reaction. Instead, there's a give and take. People naturally respond to questions, and the discussion moves along.

Or you can gently challenge their belief with a question like this: "Do you think *any* behavior is morally appropriate simply because it has a genetic link?" Notice that even though you're asking a question, you're still making your point. Just because a behavior has a genetic component, that doesn't make it right. Making your point with a question is friendlier.

Another way to incorporate questions into your conversation is to use the "burden of proof" rule. Applying this rule makes discussions about homosexuality less difficult and more engaging. The burden of proof is simply the responsibility to give proof—credible reasons—in favor of a point of view. The rule is simple: The people who offer an opinion bear the burden to give reasons for it. If they make a claim, it is their job to defend it, not yours to refute it.

Too often Christians ignore this rule. Someone says something like, "Christianity is a homophobic religion," and off we go defending ourselves. This is unnecessary. Why should we do all the work, when they made the statement? They made the claim, so it's their job to defend it.

Simply ask, "How did you come to that conclusion?" or "What reasons do you have for thinking that's true?" Then sit back and quietly listen. The question gently shifts the burden back where it belongs—on the person who made the claim. It asks them to give reasons for their view, which is a legitimate request. It also makes our job easier by taking the pressure off us to respond.

Questions allow us to make our points and advance the discussion in disarming ways. When we incorporate questions, our discussions about homosexuality become less intimidating. We can make our points without pushing our views on others. And we spend less time in the hot seat, responding to claims we have no obligation to address.

Speak It with Compassion

We need to add one more critical element to temper our approach. If we know the truth and know how to help others see it, yet we don't communicate it in a way that shows we care, we'll botch the whole thing. We need to be moved with empathy and to express that clearly. It might be difficult for us to relate to having same-sex attractions, but we've all been in tough situations and struggled with things we knew were wrong. When we're not compassionate, we come off as cold and harsh. We forget we're talking to human beings who have feelings just like us.

The combination of truth and compassion works. It's biblically consistent and cultivates healthy relationships with gays and lesbians. This is a delicate balance though. If you come on too strong with your religious views, you'll be labeled homophobic. If you get too friendly with the gay community, you'll be tagged a compromiser by someone in the church. It doesn't have to be that way. You can hold that homosexual behavior is wrong but still have a Jesus-like influence on gays and lesbians by nurturing positive relationships with them.[10]

What does it look like to speak the truth with compassion? Three principles can help us live this out practically. One, treat homosexuals as you would anyone else. Two, don't make the gospel more difficult than it is. And three, aim to make a long-term difference, not just a short-term statement.

Treat Homosexuals as You Would Anyone Else

This may seem like obvious advice, but many Christians act differently around homosexuals. They get uneasy. Their nonverbal communication, their behavior, and the direction of their conversation all change.

When gay men and women come to church, we create new rules. I remember teaching at a church that asked a lesbian to change seats because she was sitting next to another female. That's strange. I doubt this church splits up people who gossip. It's unlikely they ask unmarried couples living together to sit in different sections. Why treat a gay person any differently?

The simple answer is, we shouldn't. We should treat homosexuals as we would any other person. Show them the same dignity, kindness, and respect you would show someone who isn't gay. Here are two specific suggestions for doing this.

First, make friends with a gay man or woman. Get to know them personally, their dreams, their fears, and their challenges. Play tennis with them. Go to their social gatherings. Get to know their families and friends. Be vulnerable about your own struggles and failings. When you treat them like your other friends, they're likely to reciprocate. They'll be vulnerable too.

I know this may sound radical to some, but it's very powerful. I remember one friendship I had with a gay man. Though he knew about my Christian beliefs, I was sensitive not to bring up homosexuality unless it came up naturally in conversation. I simply focused on our friendship as I would with any other person.

Then one day *he* brought up his own doubts about the gay lifestyle. He asked me about his options. He asked me about Christianity. That's when knowing the truth—and how to defend it—really helped. We talked for hours about his lifestyle, the truth of Jesus, and where his life was headed. That kind of vulnerability and honesty is what you can expect from a real friendship. When we treat gays and lesbians like anyone else, we build relationships that create healthy intimacy. This increases our ability to make a difference in their lives.

A friend of mine made great friendships with two gay men he worked with, even though he was outspoken about his Christian convictions. He never tried to change them, confront their behavior, or hammer them about their lifestyle. Instead, he treated them like his other friends and waited patiently for an opportunity.

One day his gay friends approached him. "You're different from other Christians we know. Most harass us about being gay, but you treat us like your other friends. We appreciate that." From that point on, his relationship with them turned a corner. There was a new level of honesty in their conversation that allowed my friend to share the truth about this faith with them.

Second, don't expect homosexuals to change their lifestyle before they come to church. Several years ago, two gay men showed up to a church. They walked in, holding hands, and sat down. People next to them went ballistic. "That's disgusting," they snickered. I realize it's difficult for some believers to tolerate homosexual affection, but they should be grateful those men even came to church. Besides, gay men and women don't need to come to church *after* they're gay, but *because* they're gay. We're all guilty; we all need transformation and forgiveness. Gays and lesbians are no less welcome than gossipers and gluttons.

By treating homosexuals like anyone else, you create opportunities to speak the truth. This first principle can be put another way: When it comes to homosexuals, our desire for them is not heterosexuality, but holiness. We're not trying to make gays straight. We're trying to lead them straight to Jesus, just as we would anyone else. Once they trust Him, He transforms their life from the inside out. So to know the truth isn't merely about the truth of homosexuality—whether it's right or wrong—but the truth of Jesus and His power to transform men and women.

Don't Make the Gospel More Difficult Than It Is

"The gospel is offensive enough," Gregory Koukl of Stand to Reason says. "Don't add any more offense to it." The basic gospel message is the bad news of sin and judgment before the good news of grace. We all need a pardon. That message doesn't initially give people a warm, fuzzy feeling. In fact, it's offensive to most people. That's a big reason so many reject Jesus. We should never remove the offense that's inherent to the gospel, but there's no need to make it more difficult than it already is.

Here are a few ways we can apply this principle. First, let's stop saying we're "antihomosexual." The Bible isn't antihomosexual; it's antihomosexual *behavior.* This is a critical difference. When asked, "Are you antihomosexual?" it's better to be precise. Answer that you have nothing against homosexuals—your concern is their behavior.[11] Christians are not antidrunks. We're against drunkenness. We're not antiliars. We think lying is wrong. We're not against the person who sins. Rather, we oppose the sinful behavior. Following Jesus' example, we love and care for people regardless of their shortcomings. Saying we're antihomosexual confuses the issue and compounds an already difficult situation.

Second, let's avoid offensive ways of presenting our arguments. A common tactic to respond to the "since homosexuality is natural it must be moral" argument is to offer a counterexample. "Well, pedophilia is natural to some people, but that doesn't make it moral." Though this response might be technically sound, it is unnecessarily harsh and often misunderstood. People erroneously infer that you mean homosexuals are pedophiles. An alternative and less crass response might be to ask, "If lying to keep yourself out of trouble were natural, would that make it right?" This counterexample makes the same point without the offensive content.

Third, don't treat homosexual behavior as the most detestable crime against God. When we make it the supreme evil, we add unnecessary offense. Gays will conclude that we think all sin is bad, but their sin is the worst. And if their sin is the worst, they'll conclude *they* are the worst. But the Bible doesn't teach that homosexuality is the greatest evil. In fact, it's listed right alongside stealing, coveting, getting drunk, and lying.[12]

Next, don't call homosexuality a choice. It's not. This is hard to swallow for many Christians. Although homosexual behavior is a choice, homosexual attraction is not. I have no reason to think there's a "gay gene," but I don't believe people choose to be attracted to the same sex. Homosexual attraction is a condition that often begins to develop at a very young age—too early to be a product of choice.[13]

When you say homosexuality is a choice, this is a tip-off that you don't understand homosexuality or homosexuals. It becomes obvious you have no idea what gays and lesbians experience.

"You think it's a choice?" they ask. "Why would I ever choose to be gay? It's painful to be gay in this world. I would never choose this for myself." Not only are they offended, they'll disqualify other things you say because you don't understand them. You'll lose your ability to be an influence.

Sometimes even saying homosexual behavior is a choice will not get you off the hook because it's too easily misunderstood. The problem is, the word "choice," in this context, carries with it the idea of choosing one's sexual orientation. My suggestion is to avoid the word "choice" altogether when talking about homosexuality. It's too confusing.

Finally, avoid the cliché, "God loves the sinner, but hates the sin." It rarely gives hope to gay men and women. One former gay man confessed that he could never process this statement when Christians said it.[14] Gays don't see themselves as people who struggle with a homosexual problem. Being gay is who they are, not just what they do. Telling them that God hates their sin strikes at the core of who they perceive themselves to be. It's unhelpful and produces the opposite effect you intend.

Now that we know what not to do, let's talk about our strategy to move us forward.

Make a Long-Term Difference, Not a Short-Term Statement

I recently taught on apologetics at a university. My goal was to show how to make our message persuasive and yet gracious. After the event, I stopped at a local coffee shop for a dose of caffeine before the long drive home.

The barista served up my coffee and then asked about my day. I told her I gave a talk about how Christians can share biblical truth in a more friendly, relational, and winsome manner.

"Oh! You need to speak at *my* university," she insisted. "We're sick of 'evangelistic alley.' It's a walkway in the center of campus where Christians hold signs and yell at students. Some of them shout that God is going to judge fags. There's no discussion with them. They just want to be heard. You should teach *them*."

Though my heart sank, I realized the barista was on to something. The Christians of "evangelistic alley" were settling for a short-term goal—declaring that homosexuality was sin that should be "repented" of—while squandering their long-term opportunities. Stopping sin can be worthwhile, but it isn't the only goal. It certainly shouldn't be pursued at the expense of making a more critical, long-term impact.

The long-term plan with homosexuals should be obvious: Help them to know Christ. It's the same strategy we have with other non-Christians regardless of their sin. But it's not a quick process.[15] It rarely is with any non-Christian, but this is especially true with homosexuals. Yet we often act as if our most important goal is to change homosexual behavior in the short term rather than waiting patiently to make a more significant difference in the future.

God can give you opportunities to speak the truth with compassion anytime in a person's life. Don't try to make a moral statement today if it jeopardizes your chance of influencing people at a more opportune time tomorrow. Think long-term.[16]

One time when I was teaching at a church on homosexuality, the parents of a 25-year-old gay man asked me for advice. "He wants to bring his boyfriend over for dinner," they said, "but we told him that homosexuality is against God's design. He can come over, but his boyfriend must wait somewhere else. They need to know where we stand."

I'm sympathetic to their moral concern, but making a moral statement today might lessen their influence tomorrow. It's also unnecessary. Their son already knows their view on homosexuality. Why hurt his feelings and alienate him? There may come a time when their son is disillusioned about his life and more open to hearing the truth. If his parents have been careful not to judge and harass him unnecessarily, he's more likely to turn to them for guidance.[17] If, however, his parents have burned their bridges with him, he's not likely to turn to them for advice.

Once, while I was teaching at a church on homosexuality, the parents of a lesbian woman approached me. They were pleasantly surprised by my emphasis on truth and compassion. As they told their story, it was clear to me they were living out this principle perfectly.

Their daughter lived at a substance-abuse group home with other gays and lesbians. Every weekend the parents invited their daughter and her gay friends to their home and treated them like family. Their daughter's friends even called them Mom and Dad. Loving them was only the first step, though. These gays and lesbians needed both love and truth. So the parents invited them to church. After several months, the daughter and her friends accepted the offer because the parents showed them the kind of love and acceptance they'd expect from their own family. There wasn't a misguided attempt to make a short-term statement, only the parents' long-term plan to have an influence.

There may be times when you're asked a direct question and you have no choice but to respond in a way that sounds offensive. Sometimes that's unavoidable.[18] But we don't want to unnecessarily damage our relationship with gays and lesbians. Remember to focus on the influence you can have over the course of their life.

The Value of the New Approach

Homosexuality is here to stay. In fact, it's becoming more a part of our culture every day. Each successive generation is more accepting of the gay lifestyle. Barna's research found that "people 35 and younger are…substantially more likely to consider homosexuality an acceptable lifestyle; and notably more likely to approve of clergy conducting or blessing gay marriages." The Barna report concluded that "over the long term, we expect to see a growing acceptance of…homosexuality as Baby Busters and Mosaics, the youngest generation, become more influential in public policy and business policy."[19]

As a result, we need to know the truth and speak it with compassion more than ever.[20] Our youth will be our future leaders. They'll be our doctors, teachers, and lawyers. In 30 to 40 years, one of today's youth will be leading our country as president. The minds of young people today carry ideas that will affect our world tomorrow. Although the Barna Group's findings paint a dim picture of our future, we can brighten our prospects by reaching out to young people in the right way. We'll minimize the drastic changes that are expected in public policy as a result of the influence of pro-gay generations.

Young believers will also find this approach refreshing. Rather than being faced with the choice of keeping their faith *or* their gay friends, now they'll keep both. Their lasting friendships will give them opportunities to graciously share their convictions about homosexuality and ultimately about Jesus.

The most important reason to use this new approach is this: We know it works. It's been tried and tested. When we know the truth and speak it with compassion, we see the difference it makes. We build lasting friendships with gay men and women. We improve our chances to communicate our convictions on homosexuality. Gays and lesbians reconsider their lifestyle. And people who thought Christians only hate homosexuals now know we care.

We still have a long way to go, but our journey now has more direction. Though we're still locked and loaded, we've exchanged our bullets for truth and our clichés for compassion. Once ill-equipped to meet the challenge of homosexuality, now we're ready to answer the gay community's need for truth and healing. And though we forced Kyle back into the closet, our new approach will reach in to draw him out.

Alan Shlemon is a public speaker and writer for Stand to Reason and has been a guest on both TV and radio on the topic of homosexuality.

ABORTION AND COMMON GROUND

by Stephen Wagner

n Peter Kreeft's 1990 book *Making Choices,* he calls abortion "the most critical moral issue and moral choice of our time."[1] Yet today many people seem tired of the abortion debate, even in some circles of the church. Is the issue really relevant anymore?

Relevant Is an Understatement

A young woman studying at a Midwestern college told me her story a few years back: "I'm a Christian from a prominent Christian family in town. When I found out I was pregnant on a Monday, I considered my options and decided to have an abortion on Friday of the same week. My parents would have adopted the child. My boyfriend would have married me. But it just seemed like it was best for everyone. I'm wondering, though, if I'm mistaken to think the unborn is not a person. What's the best case you can make to me that the unborn is a person?"

This woman needed to hear a case against abortion. She wanted to hear a case against abortion. Her baby is dead because her parents, friends, and church failed to make that case to her. Each year, 1.2 million unborn children in America are killed by abortion, just like her child. The issue is obviously relevant to the children. And for every unborn child experiencing abortion, a mother and father and many others are indirectly affected by the abortion decision. God values every human being, so caring for each of these is one of the highest priorities for a healthy Christian. Most everyone is touched by abortion in some way. If that's not relevant, nothing is.

Doing Nothing Is Not Neutral

Many of us will never have to decide whether to have an abortion. But that doesn't mean the topic is unimportant for any of us. Let's apply the Good Samaritan parable to abortion. As the unborn are left for dead on the side of the road in staggering numbers, many Christians simply stumble by on the other side, just like the priest or Levite. Rather than confidently engaging the issue in a way we can be proud of, we simply neglect the issue in hope that it will go away.

That's not just a tragedy, it's a travesty.

The Abortion Issue Is a Bridge

While we're neglecting opportunities to save unborn children from abortion, we're also missing out on helping people discover the freedom of the Christian worldview. Let me be bold: The abortion issue provides one of the best opportunities to engage average Americans in dialogue on any issue of spiritual consequence. Abortion is a bridge to worldview dialogue like few other issues.

Discussing whether abortion is right or wrong leads quickly to many other questions that matter to us as Christians: Do human beings have special value? All human beings or only some? Is there a source of value that's transcendent (God)? Can we make moral claims about how other people should act? What kind of thing is a human being? Do humans sin? How can we find healing from our sin?

The issue of abortion motivates people to care about all apologetics issues. Instead of being ethereal and theoretical, apologetics begins to touch real life. The question of whether you believe in objective moral truth is no longer philosophical—it's life and death.

The Key: Engage Those Who Disagree

Conversations about abortion will never happen, though, unless Christians start speaking up. By "speaking up," I don't mean making obnoxious fools of ourselves. There's plenty of that already. I don't mean patting each other on the back for being pro-life. I mean purposefully seeking to start good dialogue with those who—*gasp!*—disagree.

One way to create dialogue is to administer a survey on a local college campus.[2] If you ask simple questions about which abortions are legal and why women get abortions, you'll find that many people just don't know the facts. If you ask specific questions about what people think of abortion at certain points in pregnancy for certain reasons, you'll find that people actually oppose many abortions. You can use the common ground built during the survey to move the dialogue forward to discuss disagreements.

Here's a common misconception: Many think that abortion is usually in response to difficult situations like rape or incest, or because the mother's life is in danger. Many people only want abortion to be legal in these cases (sometimes called the "hard cases").

In truth, most abortions are much more ordinary. What are the top three reasons for abortion today? According to the Alan Guttmacher Institute, when women were asked the most important reason for their abortions, 25 percent said they were "not ready for a child," 23 percent said they "can't afford a baby now," and 19 percent said they had "completed [their] childbearing."[3]

As you can see, these aren't the hard cases most people are so concerned about when they want to keep abortion legal (rape, incest, or the life of the mother).[4] Most abortions are social and economic. This doesn't mean that reasons like "not being ready" or "can't afford a baby" are petty. They aren't. If people argue that these are good justifications for abortion, we should first show sympathy for the women in these difficult situations. Then we can point out that we don't kill toddlers because we feel unready or too poor to care for them, so how can these be good reasons to kill human beings in an earlier stage of development (the unborn)?

Intellectual Arguments or Practical Help?

Some people wonder if logical arguments like these make any

difference. Don't pregnant women usually base their decision on practical concerns and convenience? At times, practical concerns are primary. At other times, arguments play the more important role.

The key to remember is that people are different. When you are discussing abortion (or any other issue), you need to be sensitive to the need of the person you're talking to. Some women considering abortion have a belief problem (they think the unborn is not a human being). In that case, they need apologetics. Other women have a practical problem (they may have no money to care for a child). In that case, they need the practical help of pregnancy resource centers.[5] Many times, it's both.

I've seen apologetics save the life of a girl named Kennedy.[6] I've also talked to women and men for whom apologetics didn't seem to matter. People make one of two mistakes in understanding the role of apologetics on any issue. They may dismiss it out of hand, citing a case in which someone was not helped by rational arguments. Or they may think arguments are important in every conversation no matter what. Either one size fits all, or people don't have a size at all.

Only a foolish carpenter would toss his hammer in the trash because he's doing a job that requires a saw. He will need the hammer soon enough. Apologetics arguments are like tools in your toolbox. You shouldn't throw them out because a few people are not helped by them. The next person you talk to may need them. You'd best be prepared!

Everyone Wants the Same Thing

Does anyone still care about hearing us make a case for our views? A student I met at a university in Texas is a good example of what I find on every campus. He told me he would like to believe Christianity is true, but he didn't find the evidence persuasive. Another student in Colorado said almost exactly the same thing. What an open door!

Is every student committed to truth-seeking like these two? Perhaps not, but I'd say 90 percent of the students I talk to (and I'd estimate I've talked to more than a thousand personally) are at least interested in discussing, testing, and rethinking their worldviews.

I know one thing about all the students I meet: They care about truth. It may not be the highest thing on their priority list, but it's somewhere on the list. Think about it. No one gets up in the morning and says, "I'd really like to find someone to deceive me today." I think that's a clue that we all care about truth on some level. As Christian ambassadors, our job is to reawaken in people their desire for truth on worldview issues like abortion.

Go Shoulder to Shoulder (Not Toe to Toe)

Most people haven't thought much about their beliefs, so they are overwhelmed when we ask them to reflect on their views or rethink them. Add to this the fact that the most visible people making a case for their beliefs are the strident, overconfident street preachers and talk-show hosts. If you were already overwhelmed at the prospect of thinking about your worldview, these folks really increase your tension and probably turn you off completely. Most people can't relate to a know-it-all who wants only to tell people what's true.

There is a person most people can relate to, however, and that's the Christian apologist who takes time to build common ground. The common ground attitude is inviting: "I think you're right about some things. I can learn from you." Rather than talking down to people, we're honestly placing them on our level. When I emphasize that I'm just as capable as anyone else of being mistaken, people sense that I see them as human beings and not just prizes to be won.[7] Instead of going toe-to-toe, I go shoulder-to-shoulder and turn the debate into a dialogue.

Real Common Ground

How can we build common ground? The usual approach is to toss out disagreements from the beginning. "We're not going to get anywhere with these, so let's focus on the things we can agree on." Here's how this plays out with abortion: "Let's let women make abortion decisions for themselves, and we'll focus on helping women who don't want abortions." This may sound like common ground to the pro-choice person, but it really doesn't represent the pro-life position. If I decide to stop arguing for the value of the unborn, I'm acting out the pro-choice position. That's not common ground. It's the pro-choice position dressed up in common-ground language.

My approach is different. Real common ground doesn't force people on either side to compromise their positions. So, in my book *Common Ground Without Compromise,* I offer 25 questions that most people can agree on without giving up their core beliefs. That way common ground has its proper place. We don't focus solely on a thin veneer of harmony in order to ignore the fact that we have many disagreements underneath. We engage those disagreements fearlessly, but the common ground protects the conversation from the abrasive tone many apologists have.

Engage Disagreements…How?

Do we need to be ready to make solid arguments for the pro-life position? Do we need to be ready to respond to pro-choice ideas? Absolutely. Remember the girl at the beginning of this chapter? She needed someone to make a case for the unborn. No one did. And she killed her baby.

When making your case, take note of your audience. That's another form of building common ground. If you are talking to someone who believes the Bible is the authority, argue that the Bible places humans as special among creation. Then argue that the unborn is a human being.

However, you can't assume most people believe the Bible. That's why I usually make my case against abortion with pictures, science, and philosophy. Pictures of the unborn before and after abortion clarify the facts about abortion in a way that words never can. Science demonstrates that the unborn is a living, whole organism of the human species. Philosophically, you can demonstrate that most arguments used to disqualify the unborn can also be used to disqualify those already born. Very few people think killing anyone outside the womb is okay, so these arguments are persuasive to people whether they claim to be Christians or atheists or anything in between.[8]

Notice how using pictures, science, and philosophy builds common ground with the average person today. These are sources of authority they already take seriously.

Common Ground Meets the Real World

Here's an example of how real common ground operates. I was working with a pro-life outreach project called the Justice for All exhibit on a college campus.[9] A young man I'll call Jonathan signed a poll signifying that he was opposed to the exhibit. I asked him why. Jonathan said he thought the exhibit was an eyesore. I agreed it was an eyesore (note the common ground) because it shows graphic pictures of abortions. I then asked him, "So, what do you think of abortion?"

Jonathan replied, "I don't have an opinion." So I began asking him a few of the questions from my book:

- "What do you think about late-term abortion?" (He was against it.)

- "What do you think about using abortion as birth control?" (He was against it.)

- "Do you think that as long as abortion is legal, it should be accompanied with the same safeguards as other similar surgeries?" (Of course!)

- "What about aborting female fetuses simply because they're female?" (He was definitely against that.)

- "Do you find some abortions more understandable than others?" (Yes.)

After a few more questions, Jonathan said, "I guess I have an opinion after all." Yes indeed. But if I had postured myself as someone who simply opposed him because he was pro-choice, I never would have found out how similar we already were!

Join the Conversation!

Common ground starts the conversation. Have you noticed that many people are afraid to voice an opinion on abortion or anything else because they fear being intolerant? Focusing on common ground allows them to regain their voice again.

Perhaps you feel left out of the abortion debate. Perhaps you feel it's too combative. Do you know what the debate needs? It needs ordinary people like you and me who are passionate about the unborn *and* about the people they engage. If we listen with humility, make a reasonable case with confidence, and find common ground at every step, people who disagree will engage us with interest. Then they'll start to rethink their views and question their unquestioned assumptions. That's essential if we ever want to change hearts and minds.

Stephen Wagner is the author of *Common Ground Without Compromise: 25 Questions to Create Dialogue on Abortion.* He is the director of training at Justice for All and a frequent lecturer at Focus on the Family Institute.

AN INTERVIEW WITH SKIP HEITZIG

Sean McDowell: What topics in apologetics seem to be especially relevant and important to this generation of young people?

Skip Heitzig: Worldviews—how do we know truth? How do we arrive at truth and then integrate that into a meaningful application for daily living? The God question—is there a God, and how can we know? These are issues that average church kids are asking.

Sean: Do we need to make substantial changes in our approach or content when presenting apologetics to this generation?

Skip: As far as approach is concerned, all my intel from leaders (youth especially) is telling me it's all about building a relational bridge: Build a relationship to establish trust and respect, and then dispense truth. We are presently taking that approach here on a wide scale by training 50 leaders in The Truth Project. Those 50 will then be commissioned to reproduce beyond themselves.

Sean: What advice would you give for incorporating apologetics training into the life of the church today?

Skip: Make it an ongoing staple of church life. Encourage it from the pulpit, multimedia, children's ministry, small groups, youth groups. We have our college ministry meet downtown near the university, off church grounds, for this very reason. There must be intentionality with apologetics, and it must come from the leadership. This is a huge and pressing need today—everywhere.

Skip Heitzig is the founder and senior pastor of Calvary of Albuquerque, one of America's fastest growing churches. His radio ministry airs on 400 stations and on the Internet.

DEFENDING FEMININITY:
WHY JESUS IS GOOD NEWS FOR WOMEN

by Jonalyn Grace Fincher

When I ask teenage girls and adult women what they like about being women, some rattle off stereotypical things, like makeup, buying shoes, or chivalry, but the most common response is, "I don't know what I like about being a woman."

Women inside and outside the church remain unconvinced femininity is a good thing.[1] It's time apologists realized this female confusion is worth everyone's attention. Jesus came to renew every aspect of our humanity, including our gender.[2] And in the end, gender isn't merely a woman's issue. Men are affected by women's struggles (not to mention how men are also confused about what makes them masculine, unique, and valuable).

I want to defend women's value because I follow Jesus and He valued women. Jesus wanted women to live as fully feminine, fully human, and fully free. When I got married, I realized that I had elevated one view of femininity above all others. I was surprised that my husband wanted more than my cooking skills, my home-decorating expertise, and my nurturing abilities. I expected to start a family soon, but he wanted me to finish my seminary degree and partner alongside him on the road, speaking from the same pulpits, writing in the same field. He showed me that many viable and biblical options are available for women.

My husband encouraged and propelled me into a five-year study of femininity. Along the way I've unearthed pagan ideas of femininity (and masculinity) in Bible studies, marriage conferences, men's and women's ministries, and my own prayer life. These pagan ideas, such as assuming that men and women come from different planets, or that only women are emotional or relational, or that God is male, are part of the reason women are confused about their value. If femininity only meant fashion, makeup, or cooking, we would have no problem. But these superficial earmarks of femininity are not the issue; women are actually floundering about why God would value their womanhood. This question cuts into the heart of every woman's identity, feeding a host of symptoms we'd all like to help solve: eating addiction, cutting, image obsession, premature sexualization of the female body, and pornography addiction.

Apologists can help women with our hard questions: Is there only one biblical role for women? What does Jesus really have to say about women? How does Jesus compare with other religious founders in His treatment of women?

Jesus Is a Friend of Women

Apologetics for the value of women has been done for hundreds of years. It can boast a distinguished, well-documented history, with books like Thomas Webster's *Woman: Man's Equal*—a hot topic on the eve of America granting suffrage to women. Penned in 1873, the introduction opens with these words, "Christianity is the special friend of women…This elevation is the natural outgrowth of the example and teaching of Jesus of Nazareth."[3]

Though the argument is more than 100 years old, it's worth renewing today. How do other religions—or better, how do religious founders—compare in their treatment of women? How do Islam's Muhammad, Buddhism's Gautama Siddhartha, Mormon's Joseph Smith, and Jehovah's Witnesses' C.T. Russell measure up next to Jesus of Nazareth? How fully did these founders bestow dignity on the women in their lives?

Muhammad, Founder of Islam

Muhammad (AD 570–632) could claim marital faithfulness to his first wife, Khadija, a wealthy woman 15 years his senior. But soon after her death, Muhammad married a woman each year, women of different faiths, often widows, some for family status, others for political statements, most for beauty. One of these women, Aisha, married Muhammad when she was seven but was permitted to wait until she turned nine before consummating their union. She brought her toys with her when she joined Muhammad at his home.[4]

Muhammad did act to protect females and prohibited the practice of infanticide upon baby girls. But his words about women are not always consistent:

- Regarding wayward wives: "Those whose disobedience you suspect, admonish them and send them to separate beds and beat them."

- Regarding sexual conduct: "Wives are fields to seed as you please."

- Regarding women's supposed lack of self-control: "(Wives) are prisoners with you (husbands), having no control of their person."

- Women are a distraction from prayer: "Prayers are annulled if a dog, donkey, or a woman pass in front."

- Hell is full of wives "who were ungrateful to their husbands, whose menstruation interferes with their religious duties and whose intelligence is deficient."

- "Women are the snares of the devil...Put women in an inferior position since God has done so."[5]

When I compare Muhammad to Jesus, whose female financial backers never felt the need to marry Him (Mark 15:40-41), I'm amazed at the differences. Jesus protected women and widows, not through polygamy, but through individual miracles (Mark 5:25-34), teaching (Mark 12:38-40), interpretation of the Law's meaning (Matthew 19:3-9; Mark 14:6-9), and noticing them even when they were marginalized (Mark 12:41-44).

Siddhartha Gautama, Founder of Buddhism

Siddhartha Gautama, later known as the Buddha, was a prince born near India in 563 BC. His spiritual quest led him to do two drastic things. At age 29, he awoke among his harem and realized that his concubines no longer lured him with their beauty; instead, they reminded him of a heap of corpses.[6] He left them, made one final trip to look at his wife of 12 years, Yasodhara, and their newborn son, and then abandoned everyone (harem, wife, and son) to find enlightenment. The religiously tolerant Karen Armstrong's biography of Buddha shows us that Siddhartha wasn't delighted to be a father. "He had felt no pleasure when the child was born," naming the baby boy "Rahula," or fetter. He believed the child would shackle him to a way of life he hated.[7]

Some would say that Jesus commanded us to do the same (Luke 9:57-62), but a close reading of Jesus' words reveals that He never commanded a man to leave his wife or endorsed such behavior. According to Jesus' words, a man and wife are "no longer two, but one flesh. Therefore what God has joined together, let no one separate" (Matthew 19:6 NRSV). He made no exception for spiritual quests.

Joseph Smith, Founder of Mormonism

In 1843, Joseph Smith betrayed his wife, Emma, by secretly marrying twelve women, two already married to other men. One wife, Lucy Walker, wrote an autobiographical sketch and revealed how this practice horrified her.

Joseph and Emma had agreed to care for the motherless Lucy and her brothers while their father went on mission. Lucy served as Emma's maid while going to school. When she was 15 Joseph Smith invited her to live in his home, explaining "I have a message for you.

I have been commanded of God to take another wife, and you are the woman."[8] Smith's pressure, ultimatums, and claims of a heavenly vision convinced Lucy to wed him.

Lucy's testimony is not an anomaly. In the words of Columbia's renowned historian Richard Lyman Bushman, Lucy's example is "the standard autobiography for the celestial marriage narratives in Utah."[9] Wives were separated from their husbands and friends. They were disgraced if they conceived. Most of Smith's wives were teenagers who admitted that Smith's spiritual pressure induced them to marry him.

Smith's spiritual coercion and polygamy were defended as biblical because the Bible cites several instances of polygamy. But God never commands or endorses polygamy. He does the exact opposite, commanding that the king of Israel "must not take many wives, or his heart will be led astray" (Deuteronomy 17:17 NIV). Joseph Smith records God saying just the opposite: "Abraham received concubines, and they bore him children; and it was accounted unto him for righteousness." God commands Emma to cleave to her husband and accept Smith's additional wives.[10] Jesus consistently supports monogamy. He explains that faithfulness to one spouse was God's original intentions for men and women from the beginning (see Matthew 19:4-9).

Charles Taze Russell, Founder of Jehovah's Witnesses

Charles Taze Russell (1852–1916) married Maria Frances Ackley with an agreement that their union was a marriage of celibacy for the sake of partnering in their ministry. But within a decade, Maria did not find this situation agreeable.

In their divorce proceedings, Maria testified to witnessing a sexual relationship between her husband and their foster child, Rose Ball, a teenager at the time who worked as Russell's correspondence secretary. According to Maria's testimony, Russell regularly molested Rose in 1894.[11]

Even in the socially conservative culture of late nineteenth-century America, the courts judged Russell's behavior toward his wife as "insulting," "domineering," and "improper" so as to make her life intolerable. They ruled in favor of Maria and required Russell to pay alimony.

Russell did not pay, attempting to transfer his wealth to the Watchtower Bible and Tract Society. Friends covered his bills while he fled out of state. He appealed the alimony case twice over the course of five years, eventually losing. In the end his alimony was increased.

Russell's failure to reconcile with his wife stands in stark contrast to Jesus' relationship with women of all walks of life. He wasn't wary of the Samaritan woman at the well or of the woman caught in adultery (John 4; 8). Jesus never hindered women from inheriting all He could offer them, and He allowed women to change His mind (Mark 7:24-30).

Jesus of Nazareth, Founder of Christianity

Jesus had multiple opportunities to take advantage of women. Women longed to touch Him, to serve Him, to spread their perfume on His feet, and to support Him with their money. Many men would have taken advantage of this type of female adoration. In ancient times a weakness for females was overlooked as one of the particular rights of spiritual, powerful, wealthy men. But throughout His friendships with women, Jesus refused to isolate Himself from women or to overindulge in romantic rendezvous. Women were not wicked distractions to Him, but neither were they His lovers. Instead of practicing lewdness or asceticism, Jesus guided women along the road with Him. To Martha he says, "I am the resurrection and the life...Do you believe this?" (John 11:25-26). Jesus trusted women, treating them as if they offered more to the world than their seductive charms. He permitted Mary to stay near Him and learn along with the disciples (Luke 10:38-42). He directed Mary Magdalene to preach the good news: "Go to my brothers and tell them, 'I am ascending to my Father and your Father, to my God and your God'" (John 20:17). He commended the woman who anointed His feet: "Your faith has saved you; go in peace" (Luke 7:37).

Jesus reminded the Jewish religious experts of God's original design for females. "Haven't you read…that at the beginning the Creator 'made them male and female?'" (Matthew 19:4 NIV). He is referencing the creation story: "God created man in his own image, in the image of God he created them; male and female he created them" (Genesis 1:27 NIV).

Given these four men and their treatment and teaching of women, whom would you invite to spend a day with a woman you cared about? Which religious founder would you trust with your mother, your sister, or your wife?

Blaming Women?

Though Jesus valued females, many women have never heard or learned this side of Jesus.[12] A teenage girl might survey the Christian landscape and surmise that being a woman qualifies her to go to teas or scrapbook parties but excludes her from off-roading adventures with the men's ministry. It doesn't take much to connect the dots and figure out what some churches believe men and women ought to be doing. And if this girl happens to be one of the many who do not like handicrafts, she will wonder if her femininity is some sort of liability.

A woman who is not married (through celibacy or divorce or widowhood) may find that she has no voice in her local church. Some groups even teach that young men are the key to adding members to the church. "Get the young men, the heads of households, and the women and children will follow."[13]

If this woman digs around, she will eventually learn about "the feminization of the church."[14] At its best, this topic addresses the church's failure to attract, empower, and deploy a balanced number of men and women, and men's failure to carry their share of the load. But this phrase alone might lead her to believe that too much of her sex is influencing the church. In her confusion and discouragement with her own femininity, she might protest and even get feisty. Perhaps a well-meaning older friend will tell her to have a gentle and quiet spirit. But being gentle is difficult for her when her femininity is assaulted.

Blaming women for the church's problems and humanity's problems is an ancient maneuver. Church fathers did it as early as 200 years after Jesus' resurrection, telling women to dress more modestly because, "You are the devil's gateway...you are the first deserter of the divine law...On account of your desert—that is, death—even the Son of God had to die."[15]

When women become the whipping post, I can't help but hear echoes of Adam's excuse in Eden: "The woman you put here with me—she gave me some fruit" (Genesis 3:12 NIV). Yet God created woman not to tempt or distract Adam, but to help him. In Scripture, strong men are never threatened by strong women. Quite the contrary—strong women sharpen and strengthen strong men (see Naomi and Ruth's suggestion of marriage to Boaz in Ruth 3:9, Lydia's hostessing of Paul in Acts 16:14-15, and Priscilla and Aquila's instruction to Apollos in Acts 18:24-28). Women may be made to feel as if their influence in the church were a problem, but Jesus would never make a woman feel that way. Apologist Dorothy L. Sayers explains Jesus' love for women well.

> Perhaps it is no wonder that women were first at the Cradle and last at the Cross. They had never known a man like this Man...A prophet and teacher who never...flattered or coaxed or patronized; who never made jokes about them...who took their questions and arguments seriously; who never mapped out their sphere for them, never urged them to be feminine or jeered at them for being female.[16]

If some women cannot see Jesus because of our church strategy or culture, we need to change. Female humans are not any more fallen than male humans, but sometimes by our very church practice we communicate that they are.

As Dan Kimball points out in his book *They Like Jesus but Not the Church,* many people believe that the church is dominated by males and oppresses females. Though I have been blessed with very encouraging Christian men in my life who have wanted my input, my mind, and my presence in church activities, I can see why churches can appear oppressive to females. I have witnessed leaders dismissing female opinions because they come from "women's libbers." Jesus knew that women and men reflect the wholeness of God. Both male and female must be visible, active, and influential in His church.[17]

All in the Family

Many intelligent women silence their questions because they are afraid of being called feminists. Most of these women do not have an agenda; they are honestly confused and hungry for answers. Our Scriptures include passages where women seem to be punished by God to experience pain in childbirth (Genesis 3:16), judged to be ruled by men (Genesis 3:16), relegated as weaker (1 Peter 3:7), commanded to be silent (1 Corinthians 14:34), disallowed to teach (1 Timothy 2:11-15), and instructed to call their husbands "Lord" (1 Peter 3:6), so we can cultivate understanding with those who are bewildered. Their questions are actually apologetic issues.[18]

We tell others about Christianity and Jesus by the way we treat these confused brothers and sisters. Are we willing to present our arguments for women's place in the church with equity and gentleness? Can we share many meanings to the word "head" (*kephale*), the cultural background of 1 Timothy 2, and the examples of biblical female leaders? Do we know about the Christians who allowed women to lead men, including the seventeenth-century Quakers, the nineteenth-century Fundamentalist Feminists, and today's Christians for Biblical Equality?[19] If we believe that women should not preach or serve as elders (complementarians), can we argue for this beyond stating verses without context or claiming that we feel uncomfortable when a woman preaches? If we believe women should preach and serve as elders (egalitarians), can we face verses like 1 Timothy 2:11-15 and 1 Corinthians 14:34-35 without simply saying, "It's all cultural" or asserting, "It's only fair for women to be able to preach"?[20]

The truth of the matter is that there are many biblical views of what it means to be female, not just one. Biblically sound arguments can be found on both sides, for many complementarians and many egalitarians agree that the Bible is God's inspired inerrant Word. This does not mean that God is confused about His ideas about women; it does mean that intelligent, God-fearing people do not agree. We can help those who come to us with questions when we cite another brother or sister's argument, even if we don't agree with it, as a possible biblically viable option. All these opinions are voiced in the same Christian family.

The way we talk about women's place in the home and church is an opportunity to model how Christians disagree. Let us be full of grace, truth, and humility.

Goddess Bless You?

Grian was raised in the church and attended Sunday school. As a teen, Grian taught vacation Bible school. In her Christian upbringing, Grian said her understanding of God was entirely male. She still believes that Christianity teaches that God is male.

In high school, Grian grew attracted to paganism because the goddess was more whole, more affirming to all people than the Christian's male God. The Wiccans and goddess worshippers that I have interviewed agree that the Christian God is distant, male, and unapproachable. One woman who converted from Wicca to Christianity explained to me, "The church does a very bad PR job when it comes to women. We do not generally espouse what Jesus taught. Many witches are former Christians who were never discipled beyond a rudimentary understanding of Christianity."

Jesus' resurrection reconnects women with dignity, but few Christians and even fewer Wiccans understand this. God is not ashamed to use female images to communicate His love; God cares for us like a mother (Isaiah 66:12-13); He tells Israel that He feels labor pains for them (Isaiah 42:14). Jesus even used the concept of being born again to illustrate how God is at work in the messy, intimate process of bearing us into spiritual life (John 3:3). All of these examples are biblical, helpful pictures we must learn and present to those inside and outside the church. Christians, no less than Wiccans, need to know that God is not exclusively male.

Is God Male?

The ramifications of seeing God as an exclusively male deity deeply affect young girls and their walk with God. On occasion, I've asked groups of teen girls to draw pictures of God when they've done something good. Their sketches show Jesus with arms wide open, a smiling old man on a throne, or impressions of the Trinity like three happy faces in a cluster. Then I ask then to draw a picture of God when they've sinned. They illustrate God with dark black circles or male faces with furrowed brows. One girl drew Jesus pointing to his scars. Another drew the back of a tall, male figure.

Figures with feminine characteristics are very rare, especially when girls think of God's disapproval. God, it seems, is male when they are good and especially when they are bad. I've never seen them draw from biblical pictures like God weaning his child (Psalm 131) or longing to gather us like a hen gathering little chicks (Matthew 23:37).

For most teenage girls, God is angry and male when they've sinned. Perhaps because of their own father's neglect or abandonment, young girls often cannot picture a male God being close or approachable. They could not fathom running to God when they've sinned.

If God is male, men will always share one more (rather significant) attribute with God than women will. If God is male, something about women's femininity is not suitable to be identified with God. These implications can destroy a young girl's security in her womanhood.

I am not about to say we should all call God "Mother" or that we should imagine God with breasts and be done with it. Overemphasizing God's use of female metaphors at the exclusion of the many male metaphors is not helpful or accurate. My point is that thinking of God in terms of sex leads to a dead end. God is spirit (John 4:24). God is not material; He does not have physical parts. God warned us about this in Deuteronomy 4:15-16:

> You saw no form of any kind the day the LORD spoke to
> you at Horeb out of the fire. Therefore watch yourselves very
> carefully, so that you do not become corrupt and make for
> yourselves an idol, an image of any shape, whether formed
> like a man or a woman.

Most language for God is metaphorical. The pictures help us experience truth if we can figure out where they touch reality. But every metaphor can be abused. "God is a rock" means that God is stable and strong, not that He is inert. "God is a vine" means God is the source of our life, not that He is green. When God says He is King or Judge, we learn many things about His courage and His ferocity for justice, but we know God is not male.[21] So when God says He is like a woman in labor or that Israel will be nursed (Isaiah 42:14; 66:13) we learn that God is a nurturing provider, but we know that God does not have breasts.

Today's New International Version: An Apologetic Issue

The title and metaphor for God the Father is a common stumbling block for men and women, especially if they've suffered abuse at the hand of their fathers.[22] Renée Altson, an author and poet, explains why.

> My father raped me while reciting the Lord's prayer...
>
> My father prayed with me every night. He lay on top of me,
> touched my breasts, and prayed that I would be forgiven.
>
> "Father," he said.
>
> I cringed at the association.
>
> "Heavenly Father, make my daughter a better person."[23]

To go to her Baptist church and hear God addressed as Father left Altson feeling degraded and terrified. In Bible reading and sermons, she felt dismissed as a woman—the examples were always men and fathers. "I hadn't even noticed on any conscious level how the Bible itself had excluded me. It was such a part of my life, of my memorization, of everything I was," she writes.

Years later, a priest from an Episcopal church gave her a translation like Today's New International Version. "It was as if I was reading something that included me for the first time in my life." The simple words "brothers and sisters" instead of "brothers" brought belonging to her. She suddenly mattered.[24] Altson was stunned to realize that the God of the Bible did not share her father's view of women. God wanted her to feel safe and belong in His kingdom, which is what "Father" in Scripture is meant to communicate.

I cannot relate to Altson's experience, but I think we need to pay attention to the power a TNIV Bible can have to communicate truth. We want to promote the translations that accurately include the marginalized as they are meant to be included in the original text. The TNIV, unlike gender-neutral Bibles like *The Inclusive Bible,* does not remove male pronouns like "he" or words like "King" to refer to God (contrary to much of the alarmist words on the street).[25] This means that the TNIV is a valuable tool and will offer a pivotal apologetic Bible to wounded women and men we long to reach out and comfort.

What Does Jesus Do for Women?

Simone de Beauvoir, the brilliant French existentialist and pioneering philosopher in women's studies, wrote, "It was Christianity, paradoxically, that was to proclaim, on a certain plane, the equality of man and woman...she is God's creature, redeemed by the Saviour, no less than is man: she takes her place beside the men."[26]

Jesus comes to restore all humans in the midst of our gender inferiority and gender confusion. Jesus wants to end the battle between the sexes by inviting us both into His kingdom, where "there is neither male nor female; for you are all one in Christ Jesus" (Galatians 3:28). The world's division and explanation of the battle of the sexes, including things like Venus and Mars psychology, does not agree with God's story. In Scripture we know that God made us both for the same planet, that He originally intended men and women to work together using our differences to serve one another.

I have found that Jesus, above any other religious founder, can make a real, life-changing difference to women today. He has work He wants to do in each of us. That's why I'm an apologist; I want to defend femininity the way Jesus did.

> **Jonalyn Grace Fincher** is cofounder of Soulation and the author of *Ruby Slippers: How the Soul of a Woman Brings Her Home.*

RECOMMENDED RESOURCES FOR STUDENTS

Apologetics Curricula

The Truth Project (Focus on the Family).

Rewired: A Teen Worldview Curriculum (Prison Fellowship).

I Don't Have Enough Faith to be an Atheist by Norman Geisler and Frank Turek includes a DVD series, book, and forthcoming apologetics curriculum.

The Revolt Video Series Curriculum Kit with Josh McDowell (DVD).

Lightbearers Curriculum. This is a DVD curriculum for middle school that deals with apologetic issues such as cults, moral relativism, abortion, and more.

Gospel Journey Maui. View the video trailer at www.dare2share.org/gospeljourneymaui.

Apologetics Websites

www.reasonablefaith.org. This website is based on the work of William Lane Craig. It is full of free articles, podcasts, videos, debates, and study guides.

www.str.org. This website is from Stand to Reason and is an incredible resource for apologetic questions. Greg Koukl has a dynamic radio show that he podcasts weekly.

www.probe.org. Probe Ministries is one of the most reliable, up-to-date, and relevant websites for apologetics materials.

www.allaboutgod.com. This site has tons of resources on all aspects related to building a biblical worldview.

www.pleaseconvinceme.com. This site is a wonderful resource of articles, videos, and podcasts.

www.leestrobel.com. This site includes plenty of brief video clips by experts that help explain some important aspects in apologetics.

www.soulation.org. This site provides a great example of doing a new apologetic, geared for students and adults alike, including a live chat feature for one-on-one conversations with real, live apologists.

www.TrueU.org. This is a community for college students who want to know and confidently discuss the Christian worldview.

Apologetics and Worldview Conferences

Big Dig youth apologetics conferences (www.bigdigevents.com).

Wheatstone Academy. This is one of the finest worldview conferences for students. Sessions are lead by leading scholars such as J.P. Moreland, John Mark Reynolds, and Sean McDowell (www.wheatstoneacademy.com).

Summit Ministries (www.summit.org). This is an engaging two-week summer worldview program.

Worldview Academy (www.worldview.org). Wonderful one-week summer programs take place throughout the country for high schoolers.

Apologetics Books and CDs for Students

Understanding Intelligent Design by William Dembski and Sean McDowell (Harvest House, 2008).

Smart Faith by J.P. Moreland and Mark Matlock (Navpress, 2005).

Ethix: Being Bold in a Whatever World by Sean McDowell (B&H, 2006).

The Case for Christ, The Case for Faith, The Case for a Creator, and *The Case for the Real Jesus,* all by Lee Strobel (student versions).

Living with Questions by Dale Fincher (Zondervan, 2007).

Welcome to College by Jonathan Morrow (Kregel, 2008).

Relativism: Feet Firmly Planted in Mid-Air by Francis Beckwith and Greg Koukl (Baker, 1998).

The Reason for God: Belief in an Age of Skepticism by Timothy Keller (Dutton: 2008).

Mere Christianity by C.S. Lewis.

Truth and the Real World CD set by Brett Kunkle. Includes three lectures on CD, a student workbook, and a leader's guide (in PDF form). Available at www.str.org.

NOTES

Introduction: Apologetics for a New Generation

1. Christian Smith, *Soul Searching: The Religious and Spiritual Lives of American Teenagers* (New York: Oxford University Press, 2005), 143-47.

2. J.P. Moreland, *Kingdom Triangle* (Grand Rapids, MI: Zondervan, 2007), 41.

3. I have written a critique of the "New Atheists" in the updated release of *More Than a Carpenter* (Tyndale, 2009).

4. David Berlinski, *The Devil's Delusion* (New York: Crown Forum, 2008), 50.

5. For information on the existence of a Designer, see William A. Dembski and Sean McDowell, *Understanding Intelligent Design* (Eugene, OR: Harvest House, 2008). For a recent scholarly defense of the four gospels, see Richard Bauckham, *Jesus and the Eyewitnesses* (Grand Rapids, MI: Eerdmans, 2006).

6. Robert Wuthnow, "Myths About American Religion," *Heritage Lectures,* October 18, 2007, 4. This paper can be found at www.heritage.org/Research/Religion/hl1049.cfm.

7. Dr. Richard Swenson, "Making Space in our Lives for the Things that Matter Most," presentation at Capistrano Valley Christian Schools, 2007. See www.RichardSwenson.org.

8. David Kinnaman and Gabe Lyons, *unChristian* (Grand Rapids, MI: Baker Books, 2007), 74.

9. Christian Smith, *Soul Searching: The Religious and Spiritual Lives of American Teenagers* (New York: Oxford University Press, 2005), 89.

10. Kinnamon and Lyons, *unChristian,* 81.

11. See Neil Gross and Solon Simmons, "How Religious Are America's College and University Professors?" Available online at www.wjh.harvard.edu/soc/faculty/gross/religions/pdf.

12. Alison Thomas, "Challenges from Youth" in Ravi Zacharias, ed., *Beyond Opinion* (Nashville: Thomas Nelson, 2007), 44.

13. Susan Wunderink, "Tim Keller Reasons with America," *Christianity Today,* June 2008, 39.

14. Greg Stier, "Surfing Lessons: Riding the Tricky Waves of Evangelism in a Postmodern Culture," *The Journal of Student Ministries,* March/April, 2008, 17.

15. Kinnamon and Lyons, *unChristian,* 25, 29-30.

16. Brian McLaren, *A Generous Orthodoxy* (Grand Rapids, MI: Zondervan, 2004), 31.

17. Timothy Keller, *The Reason for God* (New York: Penguin Group, 2008), 52.

18. Helen Lee, "5 Kinds of Christians: Understanding the disparity of those who call themselves Christian in America," *Leadership Journal* (Fall 2007).

19. Lee, "5 Kinds of Christians."

Chapter 2—Truth Never Gets Old

1. Nathan Rabin, "Interviews: Stephen Colbert," *A.V. Club,* January 25, 2006. Available online at www.avclub.com/content/node/44705.

2. Allan Metcalf, "Truthiness Voted 2005 Word of the Year by American Dialect Society," January 6, 2006. Available online at www.americandialect.org/Words_of_the_Year_2005.pdf.

3. The Barna Update, "Americans Are Most Likely to Base Truth on Feelings," *The Barna Group,* February 12, 2002. Available online at www.barna.org/FlexPage.aspx?Page=BarnaUpdate&BarnaUpdateID=106.

4. Brian McLaren, "Three Postmodernisms: A Short Explanation," www.brianmclaren.net/archives/000071.html.

5. Brian McLaren, "Emergent Evangelism," *Christianity Today* (November 2004), 42-43. Available online at www.christianitytoday.com/ct/2004/november/14.42.html.

6. This is a loose modern-day translation of a quote from Friedrich Nietzsche's book *Thus Spoke Zarathustra,* translated by Walter Kaufmann (New York: Penguin Books, 1966), 195. The original quote reads like this: " 'This is *my* way; where is yours?'—thus I answered those who asked me 'the way.' For *the* way—that does not exist."

7. Christian Smith, *Soul Searching: The Religious and Spiritual Lives of American Teenagers* (New York: Oxford University Press, 2005), 73.

8. Smith, *Soul Searching,* 74.

9. Smith, *Soul Searching,* 75.

10. Smith, *Soul Searching,* 143-45.

11. Joseph Ratzinger, "Homily of his Eminence Card. Joseph Ratzinger, Dean of the College of Cardinals," delivered at the Vatican Basilica on April 18, 2005.

12. Tim Johnston, "Pope assails moral relativism in Australia visit," *AP/International Herald Tribune,* July 17, 2008. Available online at www.iht.com/bin/printfriendly.php?id=14568279.

13. Adam Gorlick, "Colbert's 'truthiness' pronounced Word of the Year," *Houston Chronicle,* December 8, 2006. Available online at www.answers.com/topic/truthiness#wp-_note-12.

14. Edmund Bourne and Lorna Garano, *Coping with Anxiety* (Oakland, CA: New Harbinger Publications, 2003), viii.

15. Sean McDowell and Tony Jones, "Relativism and the Emerging Church," Sparks column in *The Journal of Student Ministries,* Jan-Feb 2007. Available online at www.conversantlife.com/relativism-and-emerging-church.

16. McDowell and Jones, "Relativism and the Emerging Church," 26-29.

17. McLaren offers this advice in a workshop entitled, "Pluralism Revisited," which I attended at the 2005 Emergent Convention in Nashville, Tennesse. Audio is available online at www.sf1000.registeredsite.com/~user1006646/miva/merchant.mv?Screen=PROD&Store_Code=YS-SD&Product_Code=NS05-029CD. A summary of McLaren's position is available online at www.brianmclaren.net/archives/2004/04/question_from_emergent_convention_32.html.

18. C.S. Lewis, *Mere Christianity* (San Francisco: HarperSanFrancisco, 2001), 32.

19. Smith, *Soul Searching,* 143.

20. Francis Beckwith and Gregory Koukl, "Truth Is a Strange Sort of Fiction—Part V: Christianity and Postmodernism: The Emerging Church," *Solid Ground,* July 2007.

21. Peter Berger, *Facing Up to Modernity: Excursions in Society, Politics, and Religion* (New York: Basic Books, 1977), 133.

22. Nancy Pearcey, *Total Truth: Liberating Christianity from Its Cultural Captivity* (Wheaton, IL: Crossway Books, 2004), 20. Pearcey's book is an in-depth analysis of the public/private split. It is a must read for Christian leaders who want to understand the thought forms that dominate the American culture.

23. Smith, *Soul Searching,* 131, 137.

24. McDowell and Jones, "Relativism and the Emerging Church." Jones charges that many Christian leaders create such straw men of relativism.

25. For your students, be clear on the distinction of knowing or being certain a statement is true (epistemological issues) and its ontological status as true (a metaphysical issue). A statement can be objectively true even if we could not know it as such.

26. Smith, *Soul Searching,* 132.

27. Smith, *Soul Searching,* 133.

28. Heather Clark, "Honestly, 'truthiness' is selected the word of 2005," *Seattle Times,* January 7, 2006.

29. This view of truth is simply assumed by Scripture. For a careful explanation of the biblical view of truth, see Douglas Groothuis, *Truth Decay* (Downers Grove, IL: InterVarsity Press, 2000), chapter 3.

30. For a summary of these trips, see www.crosswalk.com/11542880/. Or check out my newsletters at www.str.org/site/DocServer/brettkunklenews0703.pdf?docID=1789 and www.str.org/site/DocServer/brettkunklenews0508.pdf?docID=366.

31. Blaise Pascal, *Pensées,* trans. by A.J. Krailsheimer (Harmondsworth, Middlesex: Penguin, 1972), 34.

Chapter 3—A Fresh Apologetic: Relationships That Transform

1. David Kinnaman and Gabe Lyons, *unChristian: What a New Generation Really Thinks About Christianity* (Grand Rapids: Baker Books, 2007); Dan Kimball, *They Like Jesus but Not the Church* (Grand Rapids: Zondervan, 2007).

2. Christian Smith, Robert Faris, and Melinda Denton, "Mapping American Adolescent Subjective Religiosity and Attitudes of Alienation Toward Religion: A Research Report," *Sociology of Religion,* 2003.

3. Adelle M. Banks, "Study: Youth See Christians as Judgmental, Anti-Gay," *USA Today,* October 11, 2007, available online at www.usatoday.com/news/religion/2007-10-10-christians-young_N.htm?loc-interstitialskip.

4. "Un-Christian Christians," Banks, *Study;* Gary Foster, *The Foster Letter—Religious Market Update,* October 10, 2007. Available online at www.GaryDFoster.com.

5. "Hardwired to Connect: The New Scientific Case for Authoritative Communities," the Commission on Children at Risk, 2003. Copies are available to www.americanvalues.org/html/hardwired.html.

6. "Back to School 1999—National Survey of American Attitudes on Substance Abuse V: Teens and Their Parents," The Luntz Research Companies and QEV Analytics, August 1999, 4; quoted in Lori Lessner, "Dads key against drugs, study finds," *Dallas Morning News,* Aug. 31, 1999, 9A.

7. James P. McGee and Caren R. DeBernardo, "The Classroom Avenger," *The Forensic Examiner,* vol. 8, no. 5 and 6, May-June 1999.

8. Caroline Thomas and Karen Duszynski, "Closeness to Parents and the Family Constellation in a Prospective Study of Five Disease States: Suicide, Mental Illness, Malignant Tumor, Hypertension and Coronary Heart Disease," *Johns Hopkins Medical Journal,* May 1974, vol. 134, no. 5, 251-70.

Chapter 4—Christianity and Culture: Defending Our Fathers and Mothers

1. Let me suggest five good books to get you started: *The Discarded Image* by C.S. Lewis; *The Soul

of Science by Nancy Pearcey and Charles Thaxton; *Liberty or Equality* by Erik von Kuehnelt-Leddihn; *The Catholic Ethic and the Spirit of Capitalism* by Michael Novak; and *The Birth of the Modern* by Paul Johnson.

Chapter 5—A Human Apologetic: Tilling the Soul

1. When I say "imagination," I'm not talking about the activity of inventing invisible friends, as we did as kids. I'm referring to seeing things a certain way, using metaphors and story, and giving perspective to many truths we may already assume.

2. "My Very First Dad" © 1987 North Dakota Council on the Arts, as quoted in Kathleen Norris, *The Cloister Walk* (New York: Riverhead, 1997), 54.

3. This is Cornelius Plantinga's definition of "wisdom." To read more, see his book *Not the Way It's Supposed to Be: A Breviary on Sin* (Grand Rapids, MI: Eerdmans, 1995).

4. For a refreshment of these ideas see the library at Soulation (www.soulation.org). Look under "Lost Words."

Chapter 6—Capturing the Imagination Before Engaging the Mind

1. Eusebius of Caesarea, *Demonstratio Evangelica,* book 3, chapter 5, trans. by W.J. Ferrar, 1920. Available online at www.tertullian.org/fathers/eusebius_de_05_book3.htm.

2. John Warwick Montgomery, *Tractatus Logico-Theologicus* (Bonn, Germany: Verlag für Kultur und Wissenschaft, 2002), 186.

3. J.R.R. Tolkien, "On Fairy Stories;" quoted in Montgomery, *Tractatus Logico-Theologieus,* 187-88.

4. Alister E. McGrath, *Intellectuals Don't Need God* (Grand Rapids, MI: Zondervan, 1993), 194.

5. Douglas Wilson and Douglas Jones, *Angels in the Architecture* (Moscow, ID: Canon Press, 1998), 181.

6. McGrath, *Intellectuals Don't Need God,* 195.

7. McGrath, *Intellectuals Don't Need God,* 198.

Chapter 7—Conversational Apologetics: Evangelism for the New Millennium

1. This is actually one of the driving forces that led me to cowrite a book that combines apologetics and evangelism in practical ways: *Conversational Evangelism: How to Listen and Speak So You Can Be Heard* (Eugene, OR: Harvest House, 2009).

2. See Gene Veith, *Postmodern Times: A Christian Guide to Contemporary Thought and Culture* (Wheaton, IL: Crossway, 1994), 16.

3. Two examples that come into mind are when talking about issues involving evolution or morality. We need to always find ways to make our conversations sound less toxic or manipulative from others' perspective.

4. By postmodern I mean those who do not believe that one overarching story (such as Christianity) can explain the big picture. They also tend to find Christian exclusive beliefs offensive if not downright arrogant and intolerant.

5. Many secular postmoderns mix a jumble of beliefs without concern for some kind of consistency. That is why we must do more today than just deconstruct their beliefs.

6. I have talked to several people who claimed to be Buddhist and yet have admitted to me how difficult it is to live without any desire. On one occasion I said in response, "It's not just difficult

to live without desire—it's impossible. The moment you desire to stop desiring, you are still desiring something!"

7. To learn more about this approach, see our book *Conversational Evangelism* or check out our PowerPoint teaching materials at www.meeknessandtruth.org.

8. See *Conversational Evangelism* to understand more about the issues involved in uncovering real barriers to the cross.

Chapter 8—Storytelling and Persuasion

1. A proposition is a statement that affirms or denies something and is either true or false.

2. See also Proverbs 22:21-25; Zechariah 7:9-10; Romans 12:20.

3. Of course, most of the propositional content and imagery are integrated with each other, so a strictly scientific separation is not possible. Both are necessary to God's revelation, but the sheer comparison of volume is revealing.

4. I am indebted to N.T. Wright for his awesome explication of this in his two volumes, *The New Testament and the People of God* (Minneapolis, MN: Fortress Press, 1992), and *Jesus and the Victory of God* (Minneapolis, MN: Fortress Press, 1996).

5. Wright, *The New Testament and the People of God,* 77.

6. Wright, *The New Testament and the People of God,* 78.

7. Kenneth E. Bailey, *Jacob and the Prodigal: How Jesus Retold Israel's Story* (Downers Grove, IL: InterVarsity Press, 2003), 51.

8. Kevin J. Vanhoozer, *The Drama of Doctrine: A Canonical-Linguistic Approach to Christian Theology* (Louisville, KY: Westminster John Knox Press, 2005), 50.

9. Robert Gallagher and Paul Hertig, eds., *Mission in Acts: Ancient Narratives in Contemporary Context* (Maryknoll, NY: Orbis Books, 2004), 224-25.

10. Xenophon, *Memorabilia,* ch. 1. See also Plato, *Apology* 24B-C; *Euthyphro* 1C; 2B; 3B.

11. Available online at www.utexas.edu/courses/citylife/readings/cleanthes_hymn.html.

12. Sophocles, *Oedipus Tyrannus,* 260; Pausanias, *Description of Greece,* 1.17.1, quoted in Charles H. Talbert, *Reading Acts: A Literary and Theological Commentary on the Acts of the Apostles* (Macon, GA: Smyth and Helwys, 2001), 153.

13. Explained of Zeno by Plutarch in his *Moralia,* 1034B, quoted in Juhana Torkki, "The Dramatic Account of Paul's Encounter with Philosophy: An Analysis of Acts 17:16-34 with Regard to Contemporary Philosophical Debates" (Helsinki: Helsinki University Printing House, 2004), 105.

14. Euripides, frag. 968, quoted in F.F. Bruce, *Paul, Apostle of the Heart Set Free* (Cumbria, UK: Paternoster Press, 2000), 240.

15. Seneca, *Epistle* 95.47; Euripides, *Hercules* 1345-46, quoted in Talbert, *Reading Acts,* 155.

16. Seneca, *Epistle* 95.52, quoted in Michelle V. Lee, *Paul, the Stoics, and the Body of Christ* (Cambridge, UK: Cambridge University Press, 2006), 84.

17. Seneca, *Epistle* 44. 1, quoted in Talbert, *Reading Acts,* 156.

18. Dio Chrysostom, *Oration* 30.26; quoted in Talbert, *Reading Acts,* 156.

19. Epictetus, *Discourse* 1.14; quoted in A.A. Long, *Epictetus: A Stoic and Socratic Guide to Life* (Oxford, UK: Oxford University Press, 2002), 25-26.

20. Dio Chrysostom *Olympic Oration* 12:28; quoted in F.F. Bruce, *The Book of the Acts,* New International Commentary on the New Testament, rev. ed. (Grand Rapids: Eerdmans, 1988), 339.

21. Seneca *Epistle* 41.1-2, quoted in Talbert, *Reading Acts,* 156.

22. Quoted in Bruce, *The Book of the Acts,* 338-39.

23. Bruce, *The Book of the Acts,* 338-39.

24. Epictetus, *Discourses* 2.8.11-12, quoted in Gallagher and Hertig, *Mission in Acts,* 232.

25. Dio Chrysostom, *Discourses* 12.27; cf. 12.12, 16, 21, quoted in Gallagher and Hertig, *Mission in Acts,* 229.

26. Epictetus, *Discourses* 2.8.11-14, quoted in Gallagher and Hertig, *Mission in Acts,* 229.

27. Ben Witherington III, *The Acts of the Apostles: A Socio-Rhetorical Commentary* (Grand Rapids, MI: Eerdmans, 1998), 524.

28. Witherington, *The Acts of the Apostles,* 526.

29. Aeschylus, *Eumenides,* 647; quoted in Bruce, *Paul, Apostle of the Heart Set Free,* 247.

30. Curtis Chang, *Engaging Unbelief: A Captivating Strategy from Augustine to Aquinas* (Downers Grove, IL: InterVarsity Press, 2000), 26.

31. Chang, *Engaging Unbelief,* 29.

32. Chang, *Engaging Unbelief,* 30.

33. Wright, *The New Testament and the People of God,* 42.

Chapter 9—Apologetics and Emotional Development

1. These seven beliefs comprise Barna's Theolographic Profile for Evangelical Beliefs. See David Kinnaman, "Teens and Supernatural Report," 43. Available online at www.barna.org.

2. Kinnaman, "Teens and Supernatural Report."

3. "Hardwired to Connect: The New Scientific Case for Authoritative Communities," the Commission on Children at Risk, 2003. Copies are available at 222.americanvalues.org/html/hardwired/html.

4. Dr. Hall is the editor of *The Journal of Psychology and Theology* and also the founder of Alidade Research. His "Furnishing the Soul" and other work can be found at alidaderesearch.com.

5. Todd Hall, "Christian Spirituality and Mental Health," *Journal of Psychology and Christianity* 2004, vol. 23, no. 1, 66-81.

6. Will Slater, et. al., "Measuring Religion and Spirituality," *Journal of Psychology and Theology* 2001, vol. 29, no. 1, 4-21.

Chapter 11—Home-Field Advantage

1. Nehemiah Institute, Inc. "PEERS Trend Chart and Explanation," available online at www.nehemiahinstitute.com; cited in Josh McDowell and David H. Bellis, *The Last Christian Generation* (Grand Rapids, MI: Baker Books, 2006), 14.

2. "Twentysomethings Struggle to Find Their Place in Christian Churches," The Barna Update, September 24, 2003.

3. Josh McDowell, *The Relational Word* (Holiday, FL: Green Key Books, 2006), 186.

4. *The State of Our Nation's Youth,* Horatio Alger Association of Distinguished Americans, Inc., 2005. Available online at www.horatioalger.com/pdfs/state05.pdf.

5. "MTV and the Associated Press Release Landmark Study of Young People and Happiness," New York, August 20, 2007. Available online at www.mtv.com/thinkmtv/research.

6. Tim Kimmel, *Raising Truly Great Kids* conference workbook, 46.

7. McDowell, *The Last Christian Generation,* 21.

8. "Survey Describes the Ups and Downs of Tween Life," *The Barna Update,* September 30, 2006.

9. See heritagebuilders.com.

10. Exodus 10:8-11; Deuteronomy 29:10-13; 31:12; 2 Kings 23:2; 2 Chronicles 20:13; Nehemiah 8:2-3; 12:43.

11. Jerry Adler, "In Search of the Spiritual," *Newsweek,* September 5, 2005, 48-49; cited in McDowell, *The Last Christian Generation,* 34.

12. Josh McDowell, *The New Tolerance* (Wheaton, IL: Tyndale House, 1998), 174; cited in Patrick Zukeran, "Staying Christian in College." Available online at www.evidenceandanswers.org.

Chapter 12—Jesus: Risen for a New Generation

1. Also commonly referred to as the three great questions of life: Where do we come from? What is the meaning and purpose of life? And what happens when we die?

2. Thomas Oden, *The Word of Life* (New York: HarperOne, 1992), 464.

Chapter 13—Apologetics and Race

1. Timothy Keller, *The Reason for God: Belief in an Age of Skepticism* (New York: Dutton, 2008), 40-41.

2. Lamin Sanneh, *Whose Religion Is Christianity? The Gospel Beyond the West* (Grand Rapids: Eerdmans, 2003), 43.

3. Philip Jenkins, *The Next Christendom: The Coming of Global Christianity* (New York: Oxford, 2002), 2.

4. Dinesh D'Souza, *What's So Great About Christianity* (Washington DC: Regnery, 2007), 9-10.

5. Ravi Zacharias, *I Isaac, Take Thee, Rebekah: Moving from Romance to Lasting Love* (Nashville: W Publishing Group, 2004), 67, 69.

6. Curtiss Paul DeYoung, Michael O. Emerson, George Yancey, and Karen Chai Kim, *United by Faith: The Multiracial Congregation as an Answer to the Problem of Race* (New York: Oxford, 2003), 2-3.

7. Bob Roberts, *Glocalization: How Followers of Jesus Engage a Flat World* (Grand Rapids: Zondervan, 2007), 25.

Chapter 14—Homosexuality: Know the Truth and Speak It with Compassion

1. Although I use the terms "homosexual" and "gay" interchangeably in this chapter, I believe they have different meanings. "Homosexual" describes a person with predominately same-sex attractions. "Gay" is a social term to describe homosexuals who affirm the homosexual orientation as their identity. All gays are homosexual, but not all homosexuals are gay. Some homosexuals, although they have same-sex attractions, reject the gay identity.

2. Leviticus 20:13.

3. By love and grace, I don't mean agreement with the gay lifestyle. Many people like Kyle don't even get basic respect.

4. "A New Generation Expresses Its Skepticism and Frustration with Christianity," *The Barna Update,* September 24, 2007.

5. The six are Genesis 19:4-8; Leviticus 18:22; 20:13; Romans 1:26-27; 1 Corinthians 6:9-10; 1 Timothy 1:8-11.

6. Some pro-gay theology advocates suggest that the Old Testament passages that condemn homosexual behavior do not apply to New Testament Christians. Regardless of the whether this argument is valid, the Romans passage sidesteps this objection.

7. The 1 Corinthians and 1 Timothy passages merely name homosexuality as sin. Moreover, the Greek word translated "homosexuality" is a word coined by Paul and, according to pro-gay theology advocates, does not necessarily mean homosexuality (I disagree with this conclusion, however). Consequently, these New Testament passages may be reinterpreted as referring to some other sin. That's why you may save unnecessary debate by focusing on the Romans passage.

8. For a refutation of pro-gay theology, see *The Gay Gospel? How Pro-Gay Advocates Misread the Bible* by Joe Dallas. Dallas is not only a former gay man but was also involved in the pro-gay theology movement. His treatment is truthful and compassionate.

9. For an introduction in these arguments, I'd recommend *Homosexuality and the Politics of Truth* by Jeffrey Santinover, *Homosexuality and American Public Life* by Christopher Wolfe, *Marriage on Trial: The Case Against Same-sex Marriage and Parenting* by Glenn T. Stanton and Bill Maier, and articles on Stand to Reason's website, www.str.org.

10. As one who has worked hard to have a Jesus-like influence in the gay community, I can assure you I've been accused of being both homophobic and compromising at different times. One thing is for certain, you won't be able to please everyone, nor should that be your goal. I'm not suggesting you disregard everyone's feedback, but you will have to endure many unfair criticisms. Make it a priority to pray and ask for wisdom and discernment to determine how to handle each situation. You'll also need to have a group of people you can bounce ideas off of. I'd strongly recommend including people who are not only spiritually mature but also have significant knowledge or experience with this subject, such as former homosexuals, people committed to homosexual ministry, and friends or family of homosexuals. This will help you navigate difficult decisions you'll undoubtedly have to make.

11. I don't mean that homosexual thoughts, feelings, and attractions are normal or healthy. Like other thoughts and temptations, they can lead to sin. The distinction I'm making is important, though, because it helps us avoid the perception that we are against homosexual individuals.

12. 1 Corinthians 6:9-10; 1 Timothy 1:8-11.

13. I'm not suggesting people are born with homosexuality, but that it's developmental. The causes and influences happen before the child is making conscious decisions on such matters. To gain insight into factors that lead to homosexuality, read *Homosexuality and the Politics of Truth* by Jeffrey Santinover, *You Don't Have to Be Gay* by Jeff Konrad, and *A Parent's Guide to Preventing Homosexuality* by Joseph Nicolosi, or his more scholarly work, *Reparative Therapy of Male Homosexuality: A New Clinical Approach.* See also NARTH's website at www.narth.com.

14. I owe this insight to Mike Haley, head of the Homosexuality and Gender Issues Department at Focus on the Family.

15. Certainly some people turn to Jesus quickly, but this is the exception. It's more common for people to take months or years before they follow Jesus.

16. If the opportunity arises when you can make a difference in the short-term, by all means take it. Don't forsake the immediate opportunity just because you're only thinking long-term.

17. Remember, you're still likely to irritate people even if you make the right decision. Just don't irritate them unnecessarily.

18. I'm not suggesting abandoning all your convictions to accommodate everything. You still have

to stand for what is right and wrong. But take care not to needlessly alienate a gay or lesbian in your life just so things go your way. This will take discernment.

19. "Born-Again Adults Remain Firm in Opposition to Abortion and Gay Marriage," *The Barna Update,* July 23, 2001.

20. For more resources on how to live out this principle, see *God's Grace and the Homosexual Next Door: Reaching the Heart of the Gay Men and Women in Your World* by Alan Chambers and *101 Frequently Asked Questions About Homosexuality* by Mike Haley.

Chapter 15—Abortion and Common Ground

1. Peter Kreeft, *Making Choices* (Ann Arbor, MI: Servant Publications, 1990).

2. See www.STR.org/CommonGround for surveys you can print and use to create dialogue.

3. Lawrence Finer, et. al., "Reasons U.S. Women Have Abortions: Quantitative and Qualitative Perspectives," *Perspectives on Sexual and Reproductive Health,* 2005, 37(3):110-18 (table 3).

4. Less than 0.5 percent of women in the survey listed rape as the most important reason for their abortion. Four percent listed a problem with their health.

5. See www.optionline.org to find the pregnancy resource center closest to you.

6. See Steve Wagner, "Worth WAY More than a Thousand Words," *Stand to Reason Newsletter,* March 2006. Available online at www.str.org.

7. See Greg Koukl, "Gospel Fodder." Available online at www.str.org.

8. For help making your case for the unborn using pictures, science, philosophy, and the Bible, see www.stephenmwagner.com or www.str.org.

9. The JFA Exhibit runs a missions trip program that gives students the training and experience they need in order to confidently engage their world on important worldview questions. For more information, visit www.JFAweb.org.

Chapter 16—Defending Femininity: Why Jesus Is Good News for Women

1. I will be using "femininity" as a synonym for any biological or soul difference that distinguishes women from men, not merely culturally conditioned differences. For a detailed explanation of the unique aspects of the feminine soul, see my book *Ruby Slippers: How the Soul of a Woman Brings Her Home* (Grand Rapids, MI: Zondervan, 2007).

2. I will be using "gender" to mean all differences between the sexes, not as the academy uses "gender" to refer exclusively to socially conditioned differences.

3. Thomas Webster, *Woman: Man's Equal* (New York: Nelson and Phillips, 1873), introduction by Bishop Simpson. Available online at www.gutenberg.org/files/11632/11632.txt.

4. Mishkat 13, 3; Ehsan Yar-Shater, ed., *The History of al-Tabari,* vol. 9 (Albany: State University of New York Press, 1990), 131; Quoted in William E. Phipps, *Muhammad and Jesus: A Comparison of the Prophets and Their Teachings* (New York: Continuum, 1996), 142.

5. Qu'ran 2:223; 4:34; Mishkat 26, 651, as quoted in William E. Phipps, *Muhammad and Jesus: A Comparison of the Prophets and Their Teachings* (New York: Continuum, 1996), 111, 140, 148-49.

6. Samuel Bereholz and Sherab Chodzin Kohn, eds., *Entering the Stream: An Introduction to the Buddha and His Teachings* (Boston: Shambhala, 1993), 7, 9-10.

7. Karen Armstrong, *Buddha* (New York: Penguin, 2001), 1-2.

8. Lucy Walker Kimball, autobiographical sketch from the church archives of The Church of

Jesus Christ of Latter-day Saints; Quoted in Richard Lyman Bushman, *Joseph Smith: Rough Stone Rolling: A Cultural Biography of Mormonism's Founder* (New York: Alfred A. Knopf, 2005), 490-91.

9. Bushman, *Joseph Smith: Rough Stone Rolling,* 492-493.

10. Joseph Smith, *Doctrine and Covenants,* 132:37, 52-54.

11. J.J. Ross, *Some Facts and More Facts About the Self-styled Pastor Charles T. Russell* (Santa Anna, CA: Westminster Press, 1920), 25-31.

12. My husband and I have found women confused, lost, and even homeless about their femininity. But we are convinced that men are equally lost. We've seen that men tend to define their masculinity through competition, control, and disdain for women rather than through measuring themselves to Christ. The popularity of John Eldredge's books and the like indicate a vacuum in both sexes and a longing for clarity about their gender.

13. For more see Church for Men at www.churchformen.com/index.php.

14. See David Murrow, *Why Men Hate Going to Church;* Lean J. Podles, *The Church Impotent: The Feminization of Christianity;* Holly Pivec, "The Feminization of the Church," *Biola Connections,* available online at www.biola.edu/admin/connections/articles/06spring/feminization.cfm.

15. See Julia O'Faolain and Lauro Martines, eds., *Not in God's Image: Women in History from the Greeks to the Victorians* (New York: Harper Torchbooks, 1973).

16. Dorothy L. Sayers, *Are Women Human?* (Grand Rapids: Eerdmans, 1971), 68-69.

17. Dan Kimball, *They Like Jesus but Not the Church* (Grand Rapids, MI: Zondervan, 2007), 121.

18. To develop a better understanding of these verses see *The IVP Women's Bible Commentary* (Downers Grove, IL: InterVarsity Press, 2002); Sarah Sumner, *Men and Women in the Church: Building Consensus on Christian Leadership* (Downers Grove, IL: InterVarsity Press, 2003).

19. To read up on these movements I recommend Ronald Pierce and Rebecca Goouthius, eds., *Christians for Biblical Equality: Complementarity Without Hierarchy* (Downers Grove, IL: InterVarsity Press, 2005), 23-75.

20. Here are some good sources for understanding these verses: *The IVP Women's Bible Commentary, Women and Men in Ministry: A Complementary Perspective* (Chicago: Moody Press, 2001), and *Christians for Biblical Equality.*

21. Not until my postgraduate work, when I began researching God, femininity, and imagery in Scripture, did I realize that it was not Jesus' maleness that saved humans, it was His divinity. For more on this see Sumner, *Men and Women in the Church.*

22. For a man's story of this see William P. Young, *The Shack* (Newbury Park, CA: Windblown Media, 2007).

23. Renée Altson, *Stumbling Toward Faith: My Longing to Heal from the Evil that God Allowed* (Grand Rapids, MI: Zondervan Youth Specialties, 2004), 11, 15.

24. Altson, *Stumbling Toward Faith,* 155, 156.

25. See Gordon D. Fee and Mark L. Strauss' excellent guide to translations, *How to Choose a Translation for All Its Worth: A Guide to Understanding and Using Bible Versions* (Grand Rapids, MI: Zondervan, 2007), 97-108.

26. Simone de Beauvoir, *The Second Sex* (New York: Vintage Books 1989), 131, 170.

Crazy,

Beautiful,

Messed Up,

Breathtaking

World...

And People Are Talking About It...

conversant life .com

engage your faith